Start Now!

Also by Chelsea Clinton

It's Your World:
Get Informed, Get Inspired & Get Going!

She Persisted:
13 American Women Who Changed the World

She Persisted Around the World:
13 Women Who Changed History

Start Now!

You Can Make a Difference

Chelsea Clinton

Philomel Books

PHILOMEL BOOKS
an imprint of Penguin Random House LLC
375 Hudson Street, New York, NY 10014

Library of Congress Cataloging-in-Publication Data is available upon request.
Printed in the United States of America.
ISBN 9780525514367
10 9 8 7 6 5 4 3 2 1
Edited by Jill Santopolo.
Design by Jennifer Chung.
Text set in Adobe Garamond Pro.

In gratitude for every young person
who wants to change the world for the better—
and is already working to do just that

CONTENTS

INTRODUCTION

How can we take care of our planet and ourselves? How can we take care of one another and stop bullying? How can we protect endangered animals so that they don't become extinct? These are some of the questions I wondered about as a kid. I wrote this book to help readers begin to answer these and other questions kids have told me they're thinking about. I hope the information and stories in *Start Now!* will empower and inspire you to work on whatever captures your imagination. You may not be old enough yet to vote or to volunteer—but you are definitely the right age to raise your voice about important issues you care about, at home, in your school, in your community and in our world. You can help your family be healthy and make climate-smart decisions at home. You can talk to your classmates about being allies against bullying and educate friends about the importance of protecting animals around the world. You can write to your elected officials with ideas about ensuring everyone has enough food to eat, somewhere to call home, clean air to breathe and clean water to drink. There is so much you can do, and I hope this book helps you get started!

CHAPTER 1

WATER, WEATHER AND WHY WE DON'T DRINK OUR POOP

Have you ever seen a picture of our planet, Earth, taken from outer space? It looks like a big ball with blue oceans, green and brown continents, covered in parts by swirls and puffs of airy white clouds. Everything on our planet is made up of elements, like oxygen and hydrogen, that keep us alive. Our health—and the health of all of the animals we share our world with—depends on the health of the planet. And the health of our planet depends on how we take care of it.

PART I: WATER

Most of the Earth is water. We're also full of water—more than half of your body is made of it. We need fresh, clean water to wash, cook our food, brush our teeth and of course to drink. But filling our cups is more complicated than it may first seem.

The amount of water on the planet hasn't changed for a very long time. The water the dinosaurs drank, swam in and played in is the same water that today falls from the sky as rain or snow and that later turns into the groundwater we drink. That means that the water we use today was around millions of years ago!

Most of Earth's water is in our oceans. We don't drink ocean water because it's salty and would eventually dehydrate us (and we'd die). The water we drink comes from rivers, lakes, underground springs, even snowpack and glaciers. How do we make sure it's safe for us to drink?

What Is Clean Water?

Clean, safe water means water that doesn't have anything in it that can make us sick. That includes bacteria, viruses or protozoa, all germs that can cause some deadly diseases. Clean, safe water means it's free of harmful chemicals. We also need water that has no metals, like lead, that can hurt our brains or other parts of our bodies. Those are only a few examples of what is all too often found in water.

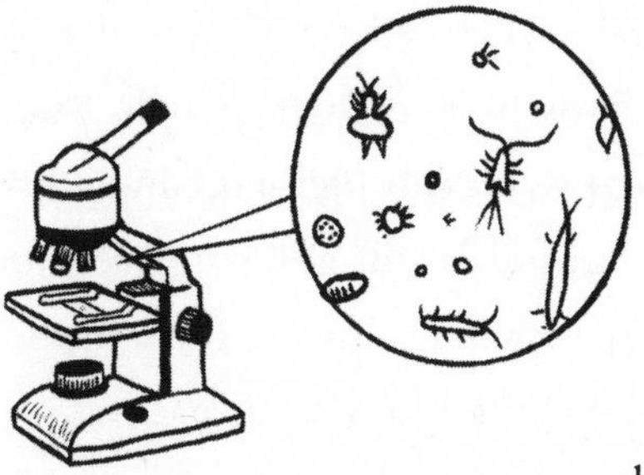

Dirty Water

Dirty water (or getting enough clean water) has always been a challenge. This is partly because so many things dissolve in water and so many other things can be carried in it. Have you ever tried to dissolve something in water? Salt (like in the oceans) dissolves in water, where it seems to disappear, even if you can still taste it.

Still, lots of things don't dissolve in water. Have you ever seen a muddy river? Or a lake with trash floating in it? The mud and trash don't dissolve in water. Neither do germs, chemicals or metals. Drinking dirty or polluted water can make us sick and even kill us. All around the world today, one out of every ten people doesn't have access to clean water. In total, that's hundreds of millions of people across the world, including some who live in the United States.

How we have purified—or cleaned—water has changed over time. Many thousands of years ago, people heated water over fire and filtered water through sand and gravel; in parts of the world today, this is still how some communities clean their water so it is safer to drink. Both the heat and the sand help kill some germs and remove dirt.

Early Water Systems

The ancient Romans were among the first plumbers! They built aqueducts—large-scale chutes—to transport water from miles away to the one million people who lived in Rome. The pipes they used were made from lead. In the Romans' language, Latin, *plumbum* meant "lead." This is where we get the word *plumbing*. (We now know that lead in water is harmful to people of all ages, particularly to kids.) These ancient Roman plumbers cleaned the water to make it taste and smell better, though it still contained dangerous germs. They also had toilets (though not as advanced as ours today) and built a sewer system to remove waste (think poop). The pipes dumped the dirty wastewater into the Tiber River, removing the bad-smelling waste but polluting the river and putting germs into the water. In part because the Romans didn't know about germs or how to kill them, this imperfect system was the best they could come up with at the time.

John Snow's Discoveries

Since Roman times, we've learned a lot about cleaning and transporting water. Still, even less than two hundred years ago, we didn't know that dirty water could make people sick.

In 1854, in London, Dr. John Snow was trying to understand how the deadly disease cholera (KAH-luh-ruh) spread. He noticed that people who drank beer were less likely to get cholera than those who mainly drank water. He then figured out that the dirty water, unlike the beer, had cholera germs in it. Snow's discovery inspired people all over the world to build systems to make water cleaner and safer.

An important improvement was having two separate systems: one for the water we drink and wash with, and one for waste that we send down the toilet. (Poop can contain germs, including cholera.) Cities and towns built modern filtration systems (that take out dirt and germs) and laid pipe systems. We learned to not dump waste back into water sources (like rivers and oceans).

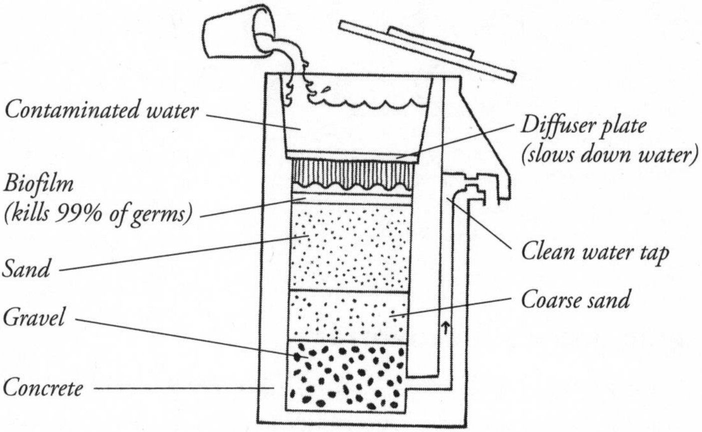

Water Treatment

In the early 1900s, cities in the U.S. and Europe began treating water with chlorine, which kills many germs, including those that cause cholera. It's similar to what is used to keep swimming pools and the water we drink today germ-free. Since water with lots of germs can stink, chlorination also helps remove bad smells. Making water safe has saved millions of lives, but millions of people today still live with dirty water. Why?

Chlorination and other water treatments are expensive.

That means that cholera and other diseases that travel in dirty water are still deadly threats in places that can't afford clean water and sanitation systems.

In many of those places, the water people drink and bathe in is full of germs, maybe even the ones that cause cholera. A single drop of water can contain millions of bacteria or viruses. Some of those germs can cause kids to have diarrhea—not just diarrhea for a day or two—painful diarrhea that doesn't go away and can be deadly. It may feel awkward or uncomfortable to read about diarrhea. But it's even worse for the many kids who have horrible diarrhea every day. Kids and their families can't avoid the germs that cause diarrhea—but they can kill them. Boiling water before drinking and washing is important in places where germs could be in the water. It doesn't remove every harmful substance, but it helps make water a lot safer to drink.

Cholera and other diseases that dirty water can carry are generally treatable. But in developing countries, many kids and families live very, very far from a doctor or health clinic. That makes clean, safe water even more important. No one should get sick from drinking water.

And, while boiling water will kill germs, it won't remove dirt or other dangers, like lead or mercury, that can lurk in water.

Bad Water in the U.S.

Bad water is a problem everywhere, even for American

cities with water and sanitation systems. A dangerous amount of lead (though to be clear, no amount of lead is "safe") has been found in the water in Flint, Michigan, and in other American communities. Some of the pipes that bring water to Flint (and other places) are made of lead, which seeps into the water—and that's a big worry, especially for little kids. Lead can hurt our brains, particularly when they are still developing and growing. Flint needs new pipes. During the wait (already too long) for new pipes, there have been important efforts to support people in Flint, including distributing water filters and bottled water.

When seven-year-old Isiah learned that people in Flint didn't have clean, safe water, he was outraged and decided to do something about it. He first thought of donating bottled water, but when his mom called an elementary school in Flint, she was told they had enough water bottles. Then Isiah reflected on all his hand-washing lessons and decided he would raise money and awareness to donate hand sanitizer to the school. He raised $25,000 and recruited a big hand-sanitizer company to donate its products. What started out as a gift to one school quickly grew. His campaign ultimately donated a two-year supply of hand sanitizer to every school and homeless shelter in Flint! Isiah lived in Virginia and had never been to Flint, but he still felt a connection to the kids there and believed no one should worry about having safe water at school (or anywhere) to use for drinking or hand-washing. I agree.

Photo courtesy of Isiah's family

Isiah with his hand sanitizer

How Much Water?

It's not only humans who need clean, safe water. Plants and animals need good water too. This means we use even more water than we think—in part because we're also eating water (as funny as that sounds) when we eat food. You can get an idea of this if you have ever squashed a grape or watered a plant in a garden—growing food uses a lot of water. But we're also wearing water (and that sounds even funnier!) because the clothes we wear rely on water.

For example, jeans are made from cotton, which needs water to grow, and that cotton is then dyed blue, a process that uses water.

If we add up all the water we use—to drink, bathe, flush toilets, wash clothes and dishes, and more—an average American adult uses eighty to one hundred gallons of water each day. That's more than three bathtubs' worth! We can all think of ways to use less water, like turning off the faucet while we brush our teeth. Some companies are working on what they can do, like creating washing machines that will use less water (and still clean clothes), while others are working on ways to cheaply turn salt water from the ocean into drinking water.

In places where families can't turn on a tap and where washing machines don't exist (because there's no electricity), even dirty water is often miles away. Those families use much less water—sometimes only five gallons of water each day, which is about one flush of a toilet. For some people, there's no clean, safe water at all. That means they're more likely to get sick—and die—from dirty water.

Digging for Water

Clean water flows underground all over the planet—but it often takes hard work to reach even the closest underground water. People have been using wells for thousands of years, and in many places (including some places in the U.S.), wells are the easiest and most reliable way to get clean water.

Photos from Matti's Walk for Water

Photos courtesy of Matti's family

When ten-year-old Matti learned that women and children, mainly girls, in Africa and Asia walk more than three and a half miles to get water every day (and then walk home again carrying the water), she knew she wanted to do something to change that. Through her church, Matti learned about a group called Living Water International that builds wells so women and girls don't have to walk so far. When women and girls don't have to walk so far, they can spend that time working or going to school instead. So, Matti, along with friends and family, organized a 3.7-mile fundraising walk in her Missouri hometown. She initially hoped to raise one hundred dollars, but over the last five years, Matti has helped raise enough money to build nine wells in seven countries.

Close to two billion people around the world still don't have clean, safe water to drink and use. That's more people than live in North America, South America and Europe combined. Efforts like Matti's are helping communities get clean water for the first time and efforts like Isiah's are protecting communities from dirty water until everyone, everywhere, has enough water to lead a healthy life.

PART II: AIR

A healthy adult can live without food maybe for weeks—and without water for a few days. But we can live only a few minutes without air. And we need clean, safe air. Just like dirty water can make us sick, dirty air can too. Thankfully, we have the power to keep our air clean, if we make the effort.

Air is 78 percent nitrogen and 21 percent oxygen. We need air to live because we need its oxygen—it is the most common element in the human body and we get it through the air we breathe. We need nitrogen too, but our bodies can't process the nitrogen in air. Plants can absorb nitrogen, so we get the nitrogen we need to help our cells grow and repair when we eat fruits and vegetables. The 1 percent of air that isn't nitrogen or oxygen contains stuff that can be harmful, particularly if we're breathing in a lot of it, over a long time.

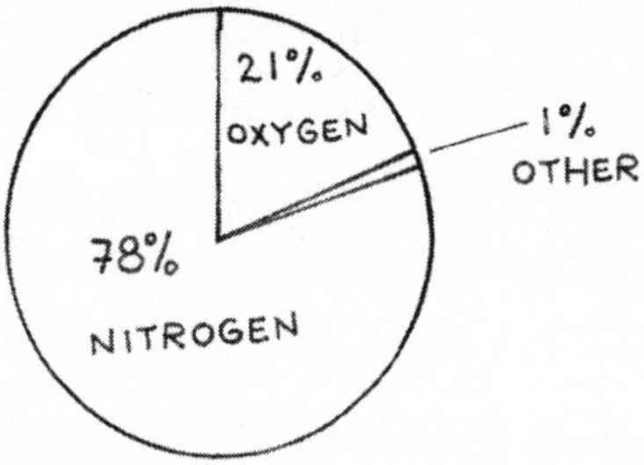

Unlike water, we can't see pure air, but we can see some of what the air carries. Think of what you've seen wind blow through the air—clouds, flowers, leaves, dust, even trash. Think of what smoke looks like from a chimney or a fire or a barbecue grill. All of that travels through the air. We can't see everything the air carries, though. When it's a muggy, humid day, the air actually has more water in it. We can't see the water, but we can feel it—the heaviness in the air is the water. When it starts to rain, we can see the rain fall through the air. So, sometimes we see the water in the air and sometimes we don't. The same is true for pollution and pollutants (the gases or particles that cause pollution). Some pollution particles are so tiny, you can only see them with a powerful microscope.

What Are Pollutants?

Just like pollution clogs the air outside our bodies, it can clog the air inside our bodies. When air is polluted, we're not just breathing in oxygen. It's the other gases and particles that can harm our hearts, our brains and especially our lungs.

Air pollutants come from many places. A lot come from fossil fuels, such as coal, oil and natural gas that are burned to power cars, airplanes and factories. Fossil fuels got their name because they formed from the fossils of plants and animals that lived a long time ago. Other air pollutants come from forest fires, volcanoes, even swamps and farmland. When we can see pollution (think of smoke coming out of a factory or exhaust from a car), we're seeing lots of particles together. Most pollutants, including carbon monoxide and carbon dioxide, are gases that we can't see, but their dangers are very real.

Carbon Monoxide

Carbon monoxide (mun-AHK-side), or CO, comes from burning coal, wood and charcoal and is in the tobacco smoke from cigarettes and cigars. If we breathe in a little carbon monoxide, it can make it harder to concentrate or pay attention. If we breathe in a lot, it can be deadly. Carbon monoxide is dangerous because it pushes oxygen out of our blood, and because it has no smell, we can't even tell it's there. Most states require carbon monoxide alarms to be in every home because it is so dangerous. You probably have one in your home.

Smog

Ever notice how the air smells after a thunderstorm? That's ozone. While that's a cool factoid, when ozone is combined with sunlight and other gases, it makes smog. Smog is a very dangerous type of pollution that makes breathing difficult, sometimes even impossible. In 1952, during the Great London Smog, thousands of people died in less than a week because they had so much trouble breathing. To make sure that would never happen again, the United Kingdom put laws in place changing how and where factories were built. The U.S. and other countries passed similar "clean air" laws to lower the levels of pollution near large cities.

Carbon Dioxide

You probably have heard of carbon dioxide (dye-AHK-side), or CO_2. While there are many sources of CO_2 (including us! that's what comes out of our lungs when we breathe out), most of the CO_2 in the air today comes from how we use energy—by burning fossil fuels. Plants take in CO_2 and release oxygen for us to breathe. In the past, our forests, plants and oceans absorbed the carbon dioxide we put into the atmosphere from our breath or the fires we burned using wood or charcoal. That's no longer true. Every year, we burn more fossil fuels and put more CO_2 in the air than the Earth can absorb.

More pollution is making us sicker. Exposure to lots of pollution at once or even lower levels of pollution over time can weaken our lungs, making it more likely that we'll get a cold or even asthma. Heavy air pollution increases the risk of lung cancer and heart disease. As important as it is to get sunlight (which provides vitamin D, which we'll talk about more in Chapter 4) and to be active, sometimes staying inside and away from pollution is the smart thing to do.

When to Stay Inside

The Air Quality Index measures air pollution. The higher the index number, the more pollution is in the air. If the index is above one hundred, it's like standing behind a car and breathing in exhaust from it all day long. Heavy traffic, a forest fire or lots of factories, particularly on a humid day, can cause the index to spike. When the Air Quality Index is high, scientists recommend that people stay indoors.

Photo and sign courtesy of Rockwood School District

The Action4Air campaign sign

An increase in ozone (meaning more ozone close to the ground) can also raise the index. If a car is running but not being driven, it's "idling." Idling cars add to ground-level ozone. A group of fourth graders in Missouri wanted the air around their school to be cleaner. They decided to tackle idling cars on and near their campus.

They started Action4Air, a campaign to encourage parents to stop idling while waiting to pick up students. Parents listened, idling dropped—so there was less pollution! The students then shared their anti-idling program with neighboring schools.

Photo and sign courtesy of Rockwood School District

Students from the Action4Air campaign

PART III: CLIMATE CHANGE

Pollution isn't just bad for our health, it's bad for our planet. It's a big cause of global warming. That means our whole Earth is getting warmer, causing huge mountains of ice—the glaciers—to melt. This is pouring more water into the oceans, which means that sea levels are rising. Extreme weather events (hurricanes, floods, fires) are getting more extreme and are happening more often. This is climate change; it means exactly what it sounds like: The climate is changing.

Over millions of years, the Earth has had big shifts in its climate. There have been multiple ice ages, when the Earth has gotten so cold that entire continents were covered in ice. For a time, the whole Earth was covered in ice. This is called the "snowball Earth" period. Even the equator—the hottest part of our planet—had ice on it, making us look like a snowball orbiting the sun. There have been some warmer periods too. Scientists believe this current period of warming is different from earlier ones because it's happening more quickly than ever before. The ten warmest years ever recorded have been in the last twenty years. Thankfully, climate change can be slowed if we all pitch in. We'll talk about what we can do at the end of this chapter.

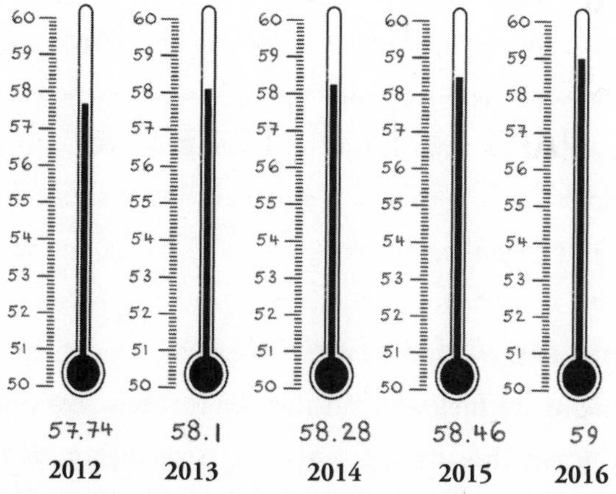

Average global temperatures in Fahrenheit over the past few years

Greenhouse Gases

One reason for our climate change has been the fast rise in greenhouse gases in our atmosphere. Have you ever seen a greenhouse? Farmers and gardeners use clear glass buildings, called greenhouses, to protect plants when the weather is too cold. Sunlight goes through the glass and warms the air, soil and plants inside. The glass is thick and hard, and stops the warm air from escaping. Like the glass in a greenhouse, greenhouse gases let sunlight through our atmosphere, then keep the warmth close to the Earth. Greenhouse gases, including carbon dioxide, make our life on Earth possible. Without some CO_2, we would all freeze—but that doesn't mean more is better. A balance is needed.

Not everywhere on Earth is getting warmer; some places are having colder and colder years. These extreme temperature shifts make it harder to grow crops, force animals out of their natural homes—their habitats—and can hurt people's health. Heat waves are extremely high temperatures that stay over days or even weeks. They are very dangerous, especially to older people and for people who cannot afford air-conditioning. Heatstroke is a dangerous heat-related injury that can hurt our hearts, our brains, and even be deadly.

Melting Ice and Warmer Water

Rising temperatures are causing ice to melt. Everywhere. Recently a chunk of ice twice the size of the island of

Manhattan broke off a glacier in Greenland. Melting ice leads to higher sea levels (because there is now more water in the oceans). All of that puts cities near oceans where millions of people live at risk of flooding from what used to be just a high tide. Warmer oceans also mean stronger tropical storms and hurricanes because storms draw more energy from warmer water. Bigger storms can ruin freshwater by turning it brackish, which means making it salty. Just like brackish water isn't good for people to drink, it's not good for watering crops. It can also kill the fish that need freshwater. Huge storms can damage homes and hurt people long after the rain and winds have stopped.

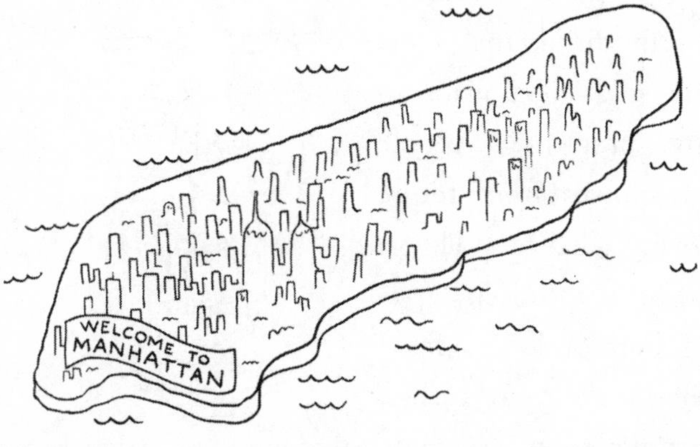

Higher temperatures and less rainfall have shrunk glaciers, which means less freshwater is flowing into lakes, streams and rivers. Hotter and drier conditions help explain why there are more wildfires in the United States and around the world.

Climate-Change Winners and Losers

Scientists talk about "winners" and "losers" from climate change. Some animals that are likely to be winners are those that can move, or migrate, to cooler climates, eat new and different food or survive in hotter temperatures. Losers are those that won't be able to move or adapt. We'll talk more about possible climate-change losers in the next chapter.

Carbon Footprint

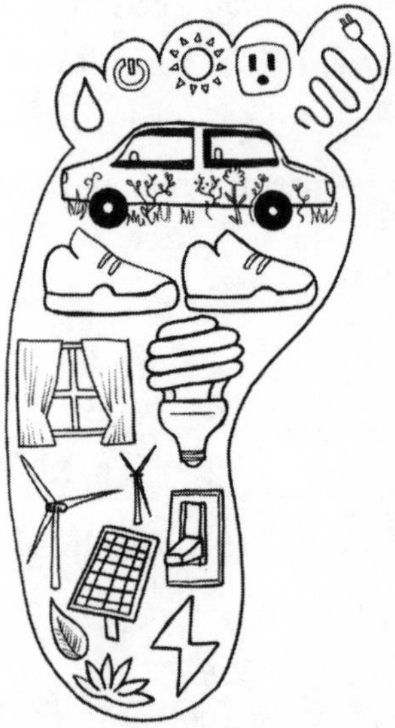

Knowing our carbon footprint, or how much carbon we put into the world, so we can shrink that footprint is a good place to start protecting people and animals from future climate change. Things that use a lot of energy—and burn a lot of fossil fuels—make your carbon footprint bigger, so activities that burn less fuel make your carbon footprint smaller. Can you walk instead of asking for a ride? Can you ask your family to buy light bulbs that use less energy? Can you unplug appliances (like lamps) or chargers (like for phones) when you're not using them? All of that can save energy. You can also talk to your teachers and neighbors and friends about climate change and organize together to reduce your carbon footprint, like the kids in Action4Air did. And you can talk to your elected officials about cutting the sources of pollution in your hometown and our country.

Recycling paper, plastic, glass and aluminum and reusing what we can, like bringing a canvas bag to the grocery store, can also save energy. If your family can afford to make choices about what food you buy, buying "local" food that is grown closer to home can also lower your carbon footprint. Food that comes from nearby didn't have to be flown or brought in on a long truck ride, and that means there wasn't as much fuel burned.

More Trees

Trees fight climate change too, by absorbing CO_2 already in the atmosphere. Right now, the world is cutting down more trees than we're planting. Trees are being cut down for lots of reasons—so that the cleared land can be used to build buildings and set up farms, and so that the wood can be used for fuel. We need to replace those trees and plant more.

Nine-year-old Felix decided the world couldn't wait for adults to fight the climate crisis. He started Plant-for-the-Planet, a program to recruit kids to plant a million trees in every country around the world. In three years, the group reached their initial goal in Germany and set a new goal: one trillion trees within ten years. One tree can absorb up to forty-eight pounds of CO_2 every year. Multiply that by one trillion. It's a lot of CO_2 that won't be in the atmosphere because of Plant-for-the-Planet's efforts. Anyone can join Plant-for-the-Planet or simply plant trees. (Just make sure any trees you plant are the right trees for that local environment.)

Felix

Photo courtesy of Felix's family

We need the fresh air and clean water of a healthy planet to keep our bodies healthy. The Earth needs us too—to use resources wisely and to protect it and all the animals and people who live here from the dangers of climate change.

START NOW! (WATER)

- Conserve water when you can by turning off the water while you're brushing your teeth or by taking a short shower instead of a bath
- Wash your hands after you go to the bathroom and before you eat
- Like Matti and Isiah, you can support efforts to get clean water to people who need it, in the U.S. and around the world
- Support clean-water efforts in the U.S., including in Flint. For Flint specifically, you can raise money for the Flint Child Health and Development Fund
- If you're worried about your water quality, ask a grown-up if they can add water-filtration systems to your taps to remove pollutants so the water is safer to use and drink
- Write to your elected officials to ask what they are doing to make sure there isn't lead in your community's plumbing, and, if there is, ask what they're doing about it

START NOW! (AIR)

- Check your local Air Quality Index number by visiting www.airnow.gov
- Support friends with asthma by playing inside when the Air Quality Index is high
- Make sure the carbon monoxide monitor in your home works
- Ask your teacher to do a science project testing the quality of your air at school or at home
- Know your carbon footprint and what you can do to reduce it
- Like Felix, you can support tree-planting efforts and even plant trees yourself. If you decide to plant trees, ask your parents to talk to a local nursery or garden store, or to use the Arbor Day Foundation's online tool to find the best types of trees for your local environment
- Raise awareness about idling and encourage your family and friends to never idle their cars

START NOW!
(OTHER CLIMATE-SMART IDEAS)

- Bring a canvas or other reusable bag whenever you go shopping
- Walk or ride your bike or scooter when you're going somewhere close to home instead of asking for a ride in the car, as long as it's safe to do so
- Ask your family to buy food that's grown near your home, if they can
- Recycle all the paper, plastic, glass and metal you use at home and at school
- Write to your elected officials to share your thoughts about climate change and what you think they should be doing to protect our environment and to ensure everyone has safe water to drink and clean air to breathe

CHAPTER 2

RHINO HORNS AND TIGER TEETH AREN'T MAGICAL

Have you heard of the dodo bird? For thousands of years, it lived on Mauritius (maw-RI-shuhs), an island country off the east coast of Africa. Dodos were about three feet tall. They had wings, but they couldn't fly. At all. They did run fast, but that didn't save them when their first predators arrived. In the 1500s, the first humans, European explorers, came to Mauritius. They brought pigs, goats, monkeys and other animals. Some of these new animals hunted and ate dodos, while others competed with dodos for food. Humans hunted dodos too. In 1681, less than two hundred years after people came to Mauritius, the last dodo was seen.

The dodo went extinct, or died out, and there will never be another again, not in the wild or in a zoo. After the dinosaurs, the dodo bird is the most famous extinct animal ever. When people say that something has "gone the way of the

A dodo bird

dodo," they mean that something is gone and is never coming back.

Animals have been going extinct forever. Scientists say that more than 99 percent of all animals that have ever lived on Earth are now extinct. That means that extinction has always been a feature of life on Earth. What's different about extinction today? We're losing more animal species and plant species than ever before.

One out of every five animals on Earth is endangered, which means that it's threatened with extinction. If nothing changes, by 2050, when you'll be around forty years old, half of all species alive today will have gone the way of the dodo.

Endangered Species— Not Just for Animal Lovers

After the dodo died out, the Calvaria tree went extinct. Dodos ate fruit from the Calvaria trees. They couldn't digest the seeds and so would poop them out, spreading Calvaria seeds around Mauritius. When there were no more dodo birds, the Calvaria trees lost the main way their seeds were dropped around the island. This meant that fewer new trees would grow. When even one species is lost, that often affects other species, sometimes leading to their extinction too.

Our lives as humans are connected to animals' and plants' lives too. There are the obvious ways, like the food we eat. There are also less obvious ways, like with certain medicines. A medicine made from the Madagascar periwinkle is used to fight leukemia, a type of cancer. Curare, a chemical taken from plants in Central and South America, is now part of medicines used in surgeries. And scientists are researching what sharks may be able to tell us about human healing and health. We don't know what other medical discoveries might be ahead, which is one of the reasons why it's important not to let species become extinct.

Since animals and plants help feed us, heal us, make our world more beautiful and enchant us with their flying, diving, jumping, dancing—why are they dying out? And what can we do?

What Used to Kill Animals and Plants

Sometimes species have died out because they lost the competition for food with other animals (or became food themselves), as happened to the dodo. Paleontologists, scientists who study fossils, believe dinosaurs died out because an asteroid, a giant piece of rock from space, hit Earth or because a massive volcano erupted. Either explosion would have created a cloud of dust so big and thick that the sun would have been blocked out, leading to a long-lasting darkness. The plants and animals that dinosaurs ate couldn't grow or survive in the dark. Without food, the dinosaurs died out too. Whatever killed the dinosaurs didn't kill all animals. Crocodiles and sharks were alive millions of years ago when dinosaurs died out, and they survived.

What's Killing Animals Today

Natural disasters, like floods, fires and volcano eruptions, can kill plants and animals, but there is no recent example of a natural disaster wiping out a whole species. Today, competition, climate change and poaching (killing animals when it's against the law) are the major threats animals face.

Competition among animals and between animals and people is growing more intense every year. Part of the reason for this is that there is less room for animals to live—their habitats are getting smaller. In some places, deforestation, or cutting down trees, is shrinking wild animals' habitats, so more animals are competing for less food and water in a smaller area. In other places, growing cities are crowding out wild animals from where they used to live and roam.

Climate change is putting pressure on animals around the world. As temperatures rise, some animals' habitats are disappearing.

Poaching is a huge threat to animals that are believed by

some people to be worth more dead than alive. Animals are killed by poachers for their meat, their skins, their tusks, their feathers and sometimes even their blood or their bones. Those dead-animal parts are then sold, sometimes only to decorate people's homes or bodies.

Around the world, more than twenty-three thousand plant and animal species are under threat of extinction. In the U.S. alone, close to fifteen hundred animal species are in danger of going extinct. You can find out about these animals and plants—and keep track of them—by looking at the IUCN Red List, which records the names of animals and plants that are in danger of extinction. The American Endangered Species List focuses on plants and animals in the United States that are in danger of dying out.

Endangered Animals Can Be Saved

We know endangered animals can be saved today and in the future because they've been saved in the past—and kids helped! In 1782, the bald eagle became the national symbol of the newly independent United States. Over the next one hundred and fifty years, bald eagles were hunted and killed by the thousands. They were forced to compete with humans for food as more and more Americans moved west. Then, in the 1940s, a new threat emerged. A chemical spray used to kill mosquitoes hurt bald eagles' ability to have eaglets (baby eagles).

By the early 1960s, there were fewer than one thousand adult bald eagles. Americans knew that if serious action wasn't taken, we could see our national symbol go extinct. The government added the bald eagle to the official endangered species list and banned, or outlawed, the chemical that was hurting bald eagles' ability to have babies. The government also started working with zoos and conservationists (people who care about protecting animals and the environment) to protect wild bald eagles and breed them for later release into the wild. Americans of all ages spoke against killing bald eagles for trophies, and against stuffing and hanging them on walls or putting them on shelves. Less than thirty years later, the bald eagle was safe from extinction and could be removed from the endangered species list.

Do you have a favorite animal? Tigers? Elephants? Giant pandas? They're all endangered. They all can be saved.

Tigers

The largest wild cat in the world, a fearsome predator, tigers are being hunted dangerously close to extinction. In a little more than a hundred years, we've lost almost all our wild tigers. In 1900, there were about one hundred thousand tigers across Asia (the only continent tigers live on natively). Today, fewer than four thousand tigers live in the wild. That means that all of the world's wild tigers would fill about ten large movie theaters (if they could fit in the seats). Although tiger moms give birth to new litters of tiger cubs around every two years, about half of all tigers born do not survive past two years old.

Tigers are under serious threat today because of poaching and habitat loss. More adult tigers are dying than cubs are being born and growing to adulthood. Poachers kill tigers because they can sell their skins for rugs or wall hangings and because tiger eyes, bones, claws and teeth are mistakenly believed to have magical healing powers. Some types of tigers are already extinct. And tigers' habitats are shrinking, in part because of deforestation. The wood for new furniture has to come from somewhere—and sometimes that's from the forests tigers call home.

Protecting tigers means protecting their habitats and protecting them from poachers in their habitats. It means teaching people that tiger bones are not going to heal or cure anything (because they can't). And it means never ever buying tiger parts. We know these efforts can make a difference for tigers because in India and Russia, they already are. With tiger reserves (areas dedicated to their protection), more rangers and stronger laws against poaching, particularly in Russia, tiger populations are growing. Russia has more Siberian tigers and India more Bengal tigers than even a few years ago.

There are more tigers in zoos and private reserves in the U.S. than there are in the wild around the world. Visiting zoos that care for their tigers and all the endangered species we talk about in this chapter is another important way to show support for conservation efforts. Every tiger deserves protection, wherever they live.

Giant Pandas

When giant pandas are born, they are tiny, pink and hairless. Hard to imagine, given how large and furry these bears grow to be. The giant panda's scientific name in Latin (*Ailuropoda melanoleuca*) translates into "black-and-white cat-foot," because early scientists weren't sure whether pandas were bears, raccoons or cats. Scientists today believe giant pandas' black-and-white coloring has helped them blend in with both shadows (the black) and snowy landscapes (the white). But it hasn't helped them escape competition with humans.

Habitat loss is the greatest threat facing giant pandas in their native China. There are even fewer giant pandas in the world than tigers, only about eighteen hundred in the wild. That makes them the rarest bears on Earth. All the wild giant pandas alive today—even if you add in the three hundred that live in panda reserves and zoos—couldn't even fill all the bleachers in some high school basketball gyms.

Giant pandas eat bamboo—and they need lots and lots of it. Some giant pandas eat up to eighty-four pounds every day—that may be around what you weigh. And they're not fast eaters, either. Giant pandas spend twelve hours or more each day eating bamboo! With more and more people in China, more forests have been cut down to make room for them to live and work. This has shrunk the natural area for giant pandas and, in some places, caused food shortages too.

The Chinese government decided to protect giant pandas. They created more giant panda reserves and limited the cutting down of trees and bamboo in giant pandas' habitats. They also stopped poachers from killing giant pandas. All of that has mattered. There are more giant pandas today than there were ten years ago.

But it's not just habitat loss that's a continued threat to giant pandas; climate change is too. Pandas are one of the few bear species that do not hibernate. That means they need bamboo all year round. Large temperature changes can kill bamboo and make it harder for new bamboo to grow. If they can't eat enough bamboo, the giant pandas starve.

Polar Bears

Polar bears are the largest bears on Earth. They have no natural predators, meaning no animals traditionally hunt polar bears. That doesn't mean they are safe. Polar bears are particularly vulnerable to climate change because of where they live and what they eat.

Polar bears live in the Arctic, a word that comes from the Greek word *arkouda*, meaning "bear." There are about twenty-five thousand polar bears spread across northern Canada, Greenland, Russia, Norway and the United States (in Alaska). While that may sound like a lot, it isn't. All the Earth's polar bears could fill maybe a quarter of the seats in a big college football stadium.

Polar bears hunt and eat seals; this is why one of their historic names was the "seal's dread." As global temperatures rise, more and more sea ice is melting. Seals live under the sea ice. With less sea ice, there are fewer seals, so polar bears must look for other food. They have to go farther and work harder for less-nutritious options. Sometimes polar bears can't find the food they need at all. When that happens, they starve, or drown if they are too tired from swimming long distances and don't have enough energy to return to the ice floes, or sheets of floating ice, where they live.

With less sea ice it's harder for pregnant polar bears to find places to build ice dens where they can give birth and keep their newborn cubs safe. To save polar bears, we need to fight climate change. As long as temperatures continue to rise, polar bears will be in danger of dying out. Some experts say if climate change isn't slowed down, by 2050, all sea ice could disappear, killing two out of every three polar bears. Every effort you make to stop climate change is helping polar bears too!

Rhinoceroses

Have you heard the expression to have "skin as thick as a rhino's"? It means being able to easily take criticism, particularly mean-spirited insults. The rhinoceros (rye-NAH-sur-uhs) does have very thick skin but its most famous feature is the horn, which gave it its name. In Greek, *rhino* means "nose" and *ceros* means "horns." Rhinos live across Africa and Asia—and poachers are killing rhinos everywhere they call home. In the last hundred years, the world has lost hundreds of thousands of rhinos. Some types, like the western black rhino in Africa and the Javan rhino in Vietnam, are gone altogether.

Unlike tigers and other animals that are hunted for their skins, rhinos are hunted mainly for their famous horns, which can be sold for more than gold. Even though it is against the law to hunt rhinos almost everywhere, poachers continue killing them because they can get so much money for rhino horns. That's because some people think that rhino horns can be used as medicine, even to cure cancer, but scientists say that's completely wrong. Yet people keep buying rhino horns for lots of money. If people didn't buy rhino horns, poachers would be much less likely to kill them. If rhino poaching continues at its current speed, scientists believe all wild African rhinos could be extinct in ten years.

Some rhinos are also in danger of losing their homes to deforestation. To save rhinos, we have to protect their habitats and protect them from poachers. We also have to continue teaching people around the world that rhino horns are not medicine. Their most famous and name-giving trait—their horns—shouldn't be their death sentence.

Pangolins

You may have never heard of pangolins. They're not native to the United States and they aren't in many American zoos. They are the animal most often illegally captured and sold, a practice called trafficking. The name *pangolin* comes from a Malay word meaning "one that rolls up." This makes sense: When threatened, pangolins roll up (and release a bad smell like a skunk does). Malay is the language of Malaysia and parts of Indonesia, Singapore, Brunei and Thailand, many of which are countries where pangolins can be found. Pangolins are also native to India, China and parts of Africa. But the fact that they live in so many countries has not protected pangolins.

Sometimes called scaly anteaters, pangolins eat mainly termites and ants, and are covered in thick scales (their nickname is "the living pinecone"). The same scales that protect pangolins from other animals are part of what makes them attractive to poachers. They are also prized for their meat, which is considered by some people to be a delicacy, or special food. There are also people who like to show off stuffed pangolins, similar to how bald eagles were showcased years ago in the U.S. And, just like rhinos and tigers, pangolins are another animal whose parts are wrongly believed to have healing powers.

Conservationists say that hundreds of thousands, maybe even millions, of pangolins are captured and sold every year, even though it is against the law everywhere to buy or sell them. To save pangolins, we need to stop the demand for pangolin meat, scales and other body parts. Pangolins are nocturnal, meaning they're awake at night and sleep during the day, and some species live in trees. That makes it harder to know where the pangolins are that need to be protected. But if poachers are finding them, conservationists can too. We can help by raising awareness about the challenges pangolins face and supporting efforts to protect them.

Orangutans

Orangutans (uh-RANG-uh-TANGS) are the largest tree-living apes on Earth. To support all their tree-climbing and swinging from branch to branch, orangutans' arms are stronger and longer than their legs. It's the opposite for people—our legs are generally a lot longer and stronger than our arms. Orangutans spend most of their lives in the forest—they build mattresses and roofs out of branches high up in trees.

Orangutan means "person of the forest" in Malay. The "person" part of their name may be because of similarities between orangutans and people—similar faces, long hair (even though many people don't have long hair, most could without haircuts!) and close relationships between baby orangutans and their moms. Given the origins of the orangutans' name, it is strikingly cruel that deforestation is the main threat to their existence.

Large parts of the orangutans' native forests have been cut for palm oil farming. Palm oil is in about half of all packaged food found in U.S. supermarkets—from peanut butter to bread to chocolate. It's even in many lipsticks and laundry detergents. Some palm oil makers have promised to stop cutting down forests where the orangutans live. That means the palm oil would then be grown sustainably—in a way that doesn't hurt the rain forests or destroy orangutans' habitats.

You can buy products made with sustainable palm oil to help protect orangutans—it might even say so on the package. That includes some Girl Scout cookies. A few years ago, Girl Scouts Rhiannon and Madison made it their mission to persuade the cookie makers to use only sustainably grown palm oil. At first, they weren't successful. But Rhiannon and Madison didn't give up. Over time, Girl

Photo courtesy of Rhiannon's and Madison's families

Rhiannon and Madison sharing their work with Dr. Jane Goodall, a famous scientist who studies orangutans

Scout–cookie makers and other companies have started using more-sustainable palm oil. Raising awareness and asking for a change may not work the first time, but it's often the first step toward progress.

Elephants

Elephants are the largest animals that live on land (blue whales in the ocean are larger). They weigh between five thousand and fifteen thousand pounds, depending on the species—that is somewhere between the size of a minivan and a city bus! Maintaining their weight means eating. A lot. Elephants eat up to four hundred pounds of food a day and drink thirty gallons of water. In comparison, adult humans are supposed to eat three to five pounds of food a day and drink eight cups, or half a gallon, of water. Elephants' most notable features—their tusks and their trunks—help them find the food and water they need. They use their tusks to dig for water (and sometimes to fight). They use their trunks to pick up food (and to give themselves a bath).

Elephants also have remarkable hearing. They can hear another elephant's call five miles away. But it's not their ears or their trunks that make them so attractive to poachers—it's their tusks, which are made of ivory.

Sometimes called white gold, elephant ivory has long been valued for piano keys, for jewelry, for religious statues and more. Ivory can be sold for hundreds or thousands of dollars. Larger chunks of ivory are generally the most valuable. The biggest tusks are found on the oldest elephants, making them a top target for poachers. When older female elephants are killed, elephant families lose more than their loved ones. Older female elephants, called matriarchs, lead their families to water, food and shelter throughout the year. Without their guidance, their families are more likely to be poached, to starve, or to die of dehydration (not enough water).

Elephants need to roam, or travel, over long distances to get all the food and water they need, leaving them vulnerable to poachers. They often leave the national parks and reserves where rangers are better able to protect them. Poachers are killing an average of ninety-six elephants a day, inside and outside protected areas. If poaching continues at the current pace, elephants could disappear in our lifetimes. If people stopped buying ivory, poachers would stop killing elephants. Many kids have spoken out to protect elephants and you can too! We need to continue teaching people that there is no safe way to remove an elephant's tusks and that elephants need their tusks to survive. Ivory always looks better on an elephant than it does on jewelry or in a statue.

Coral

When you think of coral reefs, what comes to mind? Bright, bold colors underwater? Maybe that they look like miniature forests? Sometimes they are called the rain forests of the sea. One-quarter of all ocean life lives in, on and around coral reefs. That's thousands of different species. Often thought of as plants, corals are actually animals (they're related to jellyfish). Some coral species are endangered.

The greatest threat to coral reefs is climate change. As green plants that live in the ocean absorb more carbon dioxide from the air, the ocean water changes and becomes more acidic, which is like putting a lot of lemon juice or vinegar in the water. This is not good for the animals, including fish, that live there or for the people that rely on the fish as a source of food. One effect of warmer, more acidic oceans is coral bleaching, which happens when reefs' bright colors fade to chalky white. Bleaching doesn't always kill the corals, but it often does. Once a reef dies, the fish and other wildlife that make their home there suffer too. It can take many years for reefs to recover, if they do at all. You can do your part to save the reefs and all the fish that call them home by helping to fight climate change.

In Your Neighborhood

Wherever you live, you can help protect animals and their habitats. You can teach your friends and families about why they shouldn't buy endangered species' parts, you can buy products that are made of sustainable ingredients and you can work to reduce climate change. There is a lot you can do close to home to make your own ecosystem healthier.

When ten- and fourteen-year-old brothers Devin and Roldan noticed that there were more mosquitoes where they lived in Pennsylvania than the year before, they decided to investigate. They figured out that a local swimming pool was drained every spring, killing tadpoles living there. They knew that tadpoles grow up to be frogs. And they knew what frogs like to eat—mosquitoes. How could they save the tadpoles? First, they made safe aquariums where tadpoles could grow. Then, they collected about two thousand tadpoles from the pool. When the tadpoles were baby frogs and big enough to live in the wild, Devin and Roldan released them. The result? Fewer mosquitoes and more local species, including frogs, toads, snakes and birds! The ecosystem was again in balance.

Photo courtesy of Devin and Roldan's family

Devin and Roldan helping to save frogs

Wherever you live—in a desert, near the mountains or by a lake—whether you live in a big city or a small town, you are part of an ecosystem. Work with your teachers and parents to identify which animal or plant species are important to the health of your area. Then, discover ways to protect the animals and their habitats right in your neighborhood. That's good for your community and our world.

START NOW!

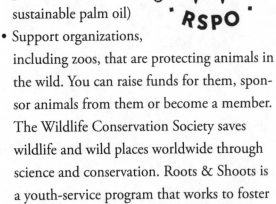

- Never buy ivory, rhino horn, pangolin scales or anything that comes from an endangered species
- Teach your family and friends that ivory only comes from dead elephants
- Tell people that there's no medical evidence that any powders or potions from dead endangered animals (like tigers) cure anything
- Encourage your parents and everyone you know to buy products that use sustainable palm oil (look for the RSPO label that proves the product only uses sustainable palm oil)
- Support organizations, including zoos, that are protecting animals in the wild. You can raise funds for them, sponsor animals from them or become a member. The Wildlife Conservation Society saves wildlife and wild places worldwide through science and conservation. Roots & Shoots is a youth-service program that works to foster respect and compassion for all living things.

There are also animal-specific organizations you can support

- Fight climate change by lowering your carbon footprint, or the amount of carbon dioxide you and your family emit
- Write letters to your elected officials about why it's important to fight climate change and protect endangered species
- Determine what you can do to help your local ecosystem, like Devin and Roldan did
- Support your local zoos, since they often provide homes for endangered species too
- Celebrate endangered animals' special days to raise awareness about the threats they face and what can be done to save them, including:
    - February 27, International Polar Bear Day
    - March 20, World Frog Day
    - April 25, World Penguin Day
    - May 1, International Save the Rhino Day
    - May 23, World Turtle Day
    - July 14, Shark Awareness Day
    - July 29, International Tiger Day
    - August 12, World Elephant Day
    - August 19, World Orangutan Day

CHAPTER 3

HEARTS, LUNGS AND WHY WE SHOULD ALL WASH OUR HANDS

Just like we have to work to keep our planet healthy, we have to work to keep ourselves healthy too! Do you remember your last checkup? Or do you know when your next checkup is? It may not be something you look forward to, but everything a doctor or nurse does at your checkup helps your body stay healthy. Why do they always listen to your chest? Ever wonder why they take your blood pressure? What about those shots—why do we need them anyway? Why does your doctor wash her hands so much? These are some of the questions you may think about when you go to the doctor. And they all have some very good answers!

In a Heartbeat

Our hearts beat about a hundred thousand times every

day—that means a little more than four thousand beats per hour, and around seventy beats every minute! Over the course of our lives, our hearts will beat more than 2.5 billion times. It is the muscle that never rests. Every day, the heart's electricity (yes, similar to what powers a light bulb!) sends enough blood around our bodies to fill about two hundred and fifty bathtubs. As our blood circulates through our body, it travels about twelve thousand miles daily—that's farther than the distance between New York City and Antarctica!

You can measure your own heartbeat by finding your pulse on the underside of your wrist and then counting how many times you feel it beat in a minute. This is called your heart rate. When your doctor puts the stethoscope to your chest, she's checking to see if your heart has a healthy rhythm.

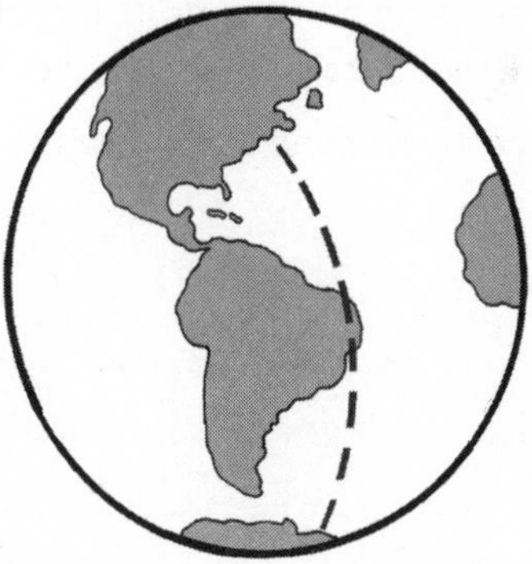

Our hearts are one of our vital organs. The others are our lungs (they bring oxygen into our bloodstream and take carbon dioxide out); our kidneys (they remove waste from our blood and make urine); our liver (it helps break down food during digestion and also processes nutrients and waste from our blood); and our brain (it enables our thinking, including your ability to read this book!).

We feel life through our hearts. A heartbeat is a life beat. Our hearts beat faster when we're excited or scared and they beat faster to help us run or jump. Without our hearts, none of that would be possible—and none of our other vital organs would work.

Is Your Heart Healthy?

Our blood pressure is another important measure of heart health, gauging how easy or hard it is for our heart to pump blood throughout our body. But you can't take your blood pressure on your own. Doctors and nurses use a cuff that squeezes your arm with a special instrument that measures your blood pressure. Most checkups include checking blood pressure.

Most babies are born heart healthy and most kids have healthy blood pressure. Our blood pressure is supposed to increase as we get older—until we're teenagers. High blood pressure, also called hypertension, is different, and means that the heart has to work harder than it should to get blood everywhere it needs to go. It can lead to a dangerous condition called atherosclerosis (a-thuh-RO-skluh-ROH-sus), when a fatty substance called plaque builds up in our arteries. (No, it's not the same plaque that can coat our teeth!) Arterial plaque starts off as a sticky deposit but, over time, it hardens—kind of like glue does—and the arteries get narrower. That makes it harder for the heart to pump the oxygen-rich blood it and other organs need. You may have heard of cholesterol. It's often a main ingredient in arterial plaque. If an artery is so full of plaque that the heart can't pump blood through it, that can cause a heart attack. If a brain doesn't get enough oxygen, that can cause a stroke. Atherosclerosis and its plaque are dangerous. Children and adults who are overweight are more likely to develop plaque in their arteries, which is one reason it's important, if we're able, to eat healthy food and exercise.

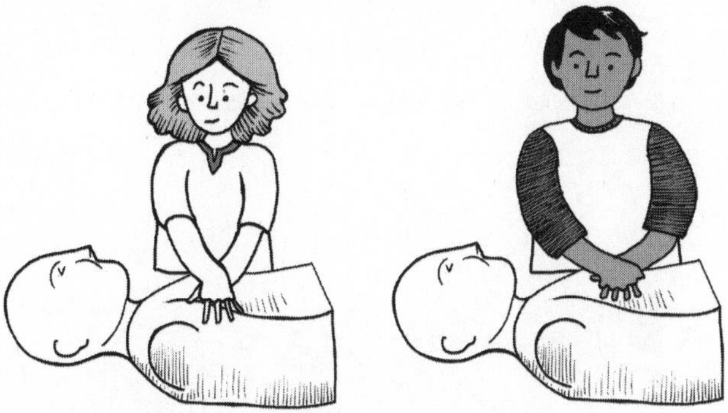

When a Heart Stops

Cardiac arrest happens when there is an electrical breakdown in the heart and the heart stops. Have you ever seen someone performing chest compressions—pushing hard and fast—on the center of someone else's chest? In real life or on television or in a movie? That is hands-only CPR, which stands for cardiopulmonary resuscitation, and it can save the life of someone in cardiac arrest. Chest compressions support the heart, quickly pumping blood to the brain so it doesn't become starved of oxygen. With training, anyone who's strong enough—including kids—can perform chest compressions, or hands-only CPR.

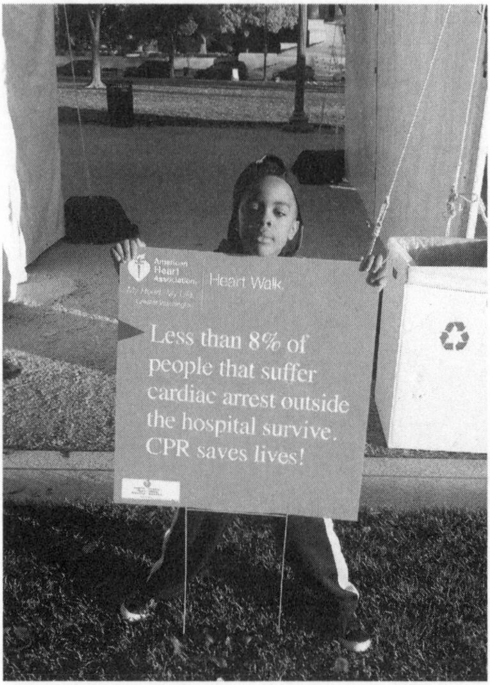

Photos courtesy of Joshua-Jaydin's family

Joshua-Jaydin with an American Heart Association sign

When five-year-old Joshua-Jaydin's heart stopped, his older brother, Keymar, was able to save his life because he knew how to do hands-only CPR, which he'd learned in school. Most kids' and adults' hearts don't suddenly stop, but learning hands-only CPR means you'll know how to save a life if someone's does.

Photos courtesy of Joshua-Jaydin's family

Joshua-Jaydin and Keymar with their mom, Monique

On the Move!

At your checkup, your doctor or nurse may have asked you to step on a scale to see how much you weigh. If we are underweight, we are more likely to get sick with things like colds, and being overweight can make it harder to breathe, harder to walk and harder for our hearts to pump. Extra weight increases the risk of diabetes (DIE-uh-BEE-tees), which we'll talk about in a few pages. The more we move our bodies and eat a nutritous diet, the more likely we'll have a healthy weight and a healthy heart.

Moving also makes us happier—that's a scientific fact! When you run, dance, jump rope, ride a bike or swim, your body releases chemicals called endorphins, which help you feel cheerful and energetic.

It's never too late to start moving—my grandmother started walking seriously in her seventies. It's also never too early. Think about babies you see wriggling around or toddlers who are so excited to walk—they run! Caleb started running when he was three, following his parents around the local track. Caleb soon ran a mile and then began to run on Sundays with his dad, over time going longer and longer distances. Now eleven, Caleb has run two half marathons (13.1-mile races) and hopes to run a marathon before he graduates from high school. He is also determined to share his love of running with everyone in his life. Caleb's elementary school participates in the 100 Mile Club, a program that inspires kids to commit to running or walking 100 miles over the school year. Caleb encourages his classmates to keep running, inspires younger students to start running and speaks at school assemblies about the school's overall running progress. Caleb now runs on Sundays with his whole family, including his younger siblings. Their support and encouragement of one another helps keep running fun—and helps keep them all running. We're more likely to stay active if we're playing, running or working out with our family and friends than by ourselves.

Caleb and his dad, Randy, after running the Cambridge Half Marathon in 2017

Eating Healthy

In addition to being on the move, what we eat is vital to keeping our bodies and hearts healthy. Our bodies are a little like cars—we both need a good energy source to run well. Just like we can measure how far a car or a bus can go on a gallon of gasoline or a battery charge, we can measure how much energy our bodies can get out of an apple or a glass of milk. All foods and drinks can be measured in calories. A calorie is a unit of energy. Something with two hundred calories has more potential energy in it than something with twenty calories. Even though that might sound like a good thing, it's not always. When we eat calories that we don't use immediately, those extras get stored as fat and too much fat isn't good for us.

The healthiest fuels for our bodies are fruits and vegetables (like apples and green beans), lean proteins (like chicken or fish or eggs or yogurt without much fat) and whole grains (like brown rice or whole-grain bread). They have fiber, vitamins and minerals that we all need to keep our bodies healthy, and they generally don't have the extra fat, added sugar or excess salt that we don't need. There are some foods that it's better for us to eat only sometimes, including fatty foods (like anything fried), food with lots of salt (like potato chips) and anything with lots of added sugar (like cookies and candy).

What we drink matters to our health too. Water is always a good choice. While water is the only thing we drink or eat that naturally has zero calories, it is vital to our health—our blood has lots of water in it. Milk, particularly the low-fat variety, is full of calcium, which kids need to build strong bones. (We'll talk more about water and calcium, plus other vitamins and minerals, in Chapter 4.)

Eating a healthy diet and playing actively are easier for

some kids than others. Families with more money can more easily buy healthier food. Kids who live in the country can probably play outside more readily. Still, most of us can try to make healthier choices. The first step is to know about the choices we're making now. How many fruits and vegetables are you eating? How many are in your refrigerator at home or your lunch at school? Do you think you need more? If yes, talk to your parents or teachers. Have you ever counted the ingredients in packaged food? Generally, the fewer ingredients listed, the healthier something is. These tips can help you figure out what healthy food you already have in your diet and what more you might need.

Dangerously Sweet

When you think of sugar, what comes to mind? Candy? Birthday cake? Apples? Broccoli? Sugar is in all of those because it's in nearly everything we eat or drink. For most people, our bodies transform sugar into fuel with the help of something called insulin. Eating too much sugar can lead to diabetes. For people with diabetes, their bodies can't effectively turn the sugar they eat into fuel. That leaves more sugar in their blood. Over time, high blood sugar can damage the heart, kidneys, eyes, nerves and feet.

There are two types of diabetes: Type 1 diabetes is when our bodies don't make enough insulin. Kids and adults with Type 1 diabetes need to take insulin, monitor their blood sugar, watch what they eat and exercise. Kids with Type 1 diabetes can play sports, have fun with their friends and lead healthy lives. Type 2 diabetes occurs when someone's insulin doesn't work well enough and their blood sugar gets high; it is often tied to eating too much sugar. With the right diet, blood sugar monitoring and exercise, people with Type 2 diabetes can lead healthy lives, and even reverse their Type 2 diabetes.

Someone helping her family make healthier—and tastier—choices is Haile. When her dad was diagnosed with Type 2 diabetes, seven-year-old Haile decided to learn to cook healthy foods, a choice her parents supported. Eating Haile's food and exercising helped her dad achieve and maintain a healthy weight, reverse his diabetes diagnosis and generally feel better. Ten years after she first started cooking, Haile is still making nutritious meals for her family—and teaching other kids and families to be healthier through kids' summer cooking camps, school programs and YouTube videos.

Photo courtesy of Haile's family

Haile cooking

Healthy Lungs: Breathing Easy

Remember the stethoscope doctors use to listen to our hearts? They also use stethoscopes to listen to our lungs and check whether we are breathing easily. For someone with asthma, breathing can be hard. You or someone you know may have asthma and you may have seen someone use an inhaler to make breathing easier—maybe you use one yourself. Lots of different "triggers" can lead to asthma attacks, including dust, cigarette smoke and pollution.

Even without asthma, no amount of cigarette smoke is safe. It's not like fat or sugar where we need healthy fats and sugars to fuel our bodies. We don't need cigarettes or their main ingredient, tobacco; a little can hurt us a lot. Someone who smokes is more likely to have unhealthy lungs, and be at risk for lung cancer. To keep our hearts and our lungs healthy, it's important we don't start using tobacco and that we encourage those around us who use tobacco in any form to quit. That's good for their health and for ours. Even breathing in smoke from other people's cigarettes, what's called secondhand smoke, can hurt our lungs—and our hearts.

Infectious Diseases

Has your whole class ever been sick with the flu or a cold or a stomach bug? Maybe not at the same time but over a few weeks? Illnesses we can catch from other people are called infectious diseases and are generally caused by germs, including viruses and bacteria. They spread when we sneeze or cough on someone (which is why it's important to cover your nose and mouth!). Germs also spread when water or food is contaminated (dirty), or when insects or other animals bite one person and take their blood and then bite another person. That's how mosquitoes, ticks and fleas pass along diseases. (Don't worry—most bug bites won't make you sick, they'll just make you itchy.)

Infectious diseases have been around for a very long time. A nine-thousand-year-old skeleton showed evidence of tuberculosis. Today, in some countries, many kids still die from infections, including tuberculosis. Thankfully, every year, more and more kids are living longer and healthier lives, in part because of cleaner water, safer food and better medicine, including vaccines.

Give It a Shot!

Do you know anyone who thinks shots are fun? Probably

not. Vaccinations (VAK-suh-NAY-shuhns) are shots that contain vaccines, small bits of a germ that's either weakened or dead. They're so important because they protect us from terrible, even deadly, diseases. How? Well, our bodies respond to the weakened or dead germs by making specific antibodies. Those antibodies then become part of our bodies, waiting to fight off live germ attacks. This process is called immunity. Hopefully our bodies never need them, but if a germ tries to invade, the antibody fighters are ready to go into action to beat back that disease. Sometimes we can still get a disease we've been vaccinated against (like whooping cough or measles), but that's rare and, when it happens, it's usually a mild, or not very bad, case of it. In the U.S., we generally receive our first vaccine as newborn babies and then we get a series of shots at checkups. Children who haven't gotten their shots are unvaccinated and are more likely to get sick from the diseases vaccines guard against.

Some vaccines have been so effective, they've made a disease very rare, or gotten rid of it altogether. Smallpox was a terrible disease that gave people painful sores all over their bodies and was especially dangerous for kids; *pox* is another word for "sore." Those who did survive smallpox were left with scars, sometimes over their eyes, leaving them blind. There was a worldwide effort to vaccinate everyone against smallpox. And now it's gone! The last case was forty years ago.

James Phipps: The Boy Who Helped Create the First Vaccine

In 1796, in England, Dr. Edward Jenner inserted a small bit of cowpox virus under the skin of eight-year-old James Phipps. Cowpox is similar to smallpox but much less dangerous. The doctor had noticed that young women who milked cows did not catch smallpox when almost everyone else did. He wondered: Did having contact with cowpox protect milkmaids from the deadly smallpox?

Dr. Jenner had believed James's body would make antibodies, helping James develop an immunity, or natural defense, against cowpox *and* smallpox. To test that theory, Dr. Jenner later inserted cowpox under James's skin. James didn't develop smallpox, and Dr. Jenner is credited with developing the first vaccine (though technically what Dr. Jenner did was called variolation). There's some evidence that Greek, Chinese and Turkish doctors developed vaccines even earlier!

George Washington and a Revolutionary Vaccine

During the American Revolutionary War, General George Washington wanted to keep his troops safe from smallpox. As a boy, Washington got smallpox and he knew how painful it was. As a general, he believed smallpox could be a greater threat than "the Sword of the Enemy." Continental army soldiers had small amounts of smallpox put underneath their skin; this was more dangerous than using cowpox, but it worked! Soldiers generally got a mild case of smallpox that, once they had recovered, left them with antibodies to protect against more serious cases. Some historians believe Washington's decision helped the United States win the Revolutionary War.

Just like there were people who disagreed with Washington's decision to inoculate his soldiers, some adults today refuse to vaccinate themselves or their children. But scientists agree: Vaccines are safe, effective and life-saving.

Antibiotics Kill (Some) Germs

If you've ever gotten an ear infection or strep throat, your doctor may have prescribed an antibiotic, a type of medicine you take for a week or so to fight off the infection and help you get better. Or if you've scraped your knee, you might have applied an antibiotic ointment along with a bandage. Antibiotics kill germs, specifically bacteria (we don't use antibiotics to treat viruses). Antibiotics are a big reason why we're less likely than our ancestors to die of infectious diseases. By peering into your throat or your ear, a doctor or nurse can often tell if an antibiotic will help you. Antibiotics have been around for even less time than vaccines; Dr. Alexander Fleming discovered penicillin, the first antibiotic, in 1928.

Florence Nightingale Made Hospitals Better

Did you notice that your doctor washed her hands before and after examining you? There are probably signs in your school reminding you to wash your hands. There are similar signs in hospitals and doctors' offices. There are lots of germs in hospitals—because there are lots of sick people. Hand-washing prevents germs from spreading. While that may seem obvious now, for a long time, it wasn't.

In 1854, English nurse Florence Nightingale went to Turkey to help take care of British soldiers who had been injured in fighting nearby. When she arrived, she found many injured soldiers were forced to share beds and blankets. There also wasn't enough medicine, healthy food or clean water. More soldiers were dying from infections and disease than from battle injuries.

Nurse Nightingale and the nurses she brought with her first cleaned the hospital, built safer latrines (a type of toilet) and got the soldiers more blankets and better food. She then persuaded the British army to build a larger hospital with more beds, better toilets and better ventilation, so air could move around and germs wouldn't stay in one place. She also introduced routine hand-washing. The number of deaths dropped dramatically. We can thank Florence Nightingale for helping to teach all of us—especially in hospitals—how to send germs down the drain. It may sound strange, but washing our hands helps us live longer!

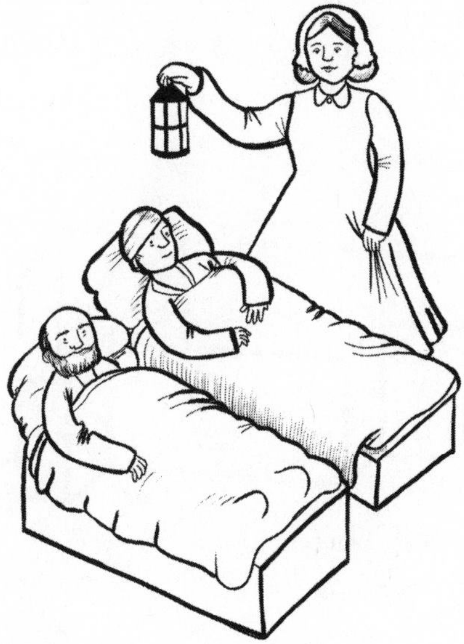

Living Longer

How long we can expect to live is called life expectancy. For thousands of years, most people lived to be about thirty to forty years old. Then, about two hundred years ago, that started to change in Europe and North America; people started living longer.

Today, most people born in the U.S. have a life expectancy of seventy to eighty years. How did that happen? Lots of hand-washing (with soap), vaccines, antibiotics and other medicines, cleaner water and safer food all have helped us be healthier and live longer. More and better-trained doctors, nurses and midwives (who specialize in delivering babies), along with more and better hospitals, help us recover when we're sick and bring babies safely into the world. Better ventilation and more space in houses and buildings have lowered the risk of both infectious diseases and fires spreading. All of that has contributed to improving our life expectancy.

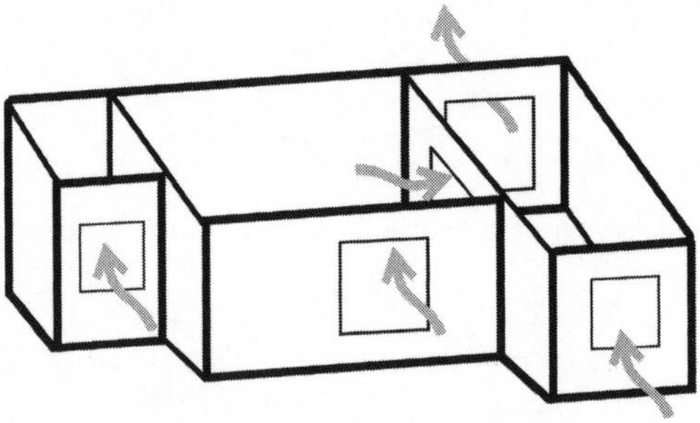

The arrows show how air moves through a well-ventilated space

Who Lives Longer and Why

Improving life expectancy did not happen everywhere, for everyone, at the same time. Wealthier countries could spend more money to discover medicines, train doctors and nurses, construct hospitals and build clean water and sewer systems (so that poop and all its germs didn't mix with drinking water). Wealthier people in those countries were more able to buy new medicines, pay to see a doctor and afford a well-ventilated home. Wealthier people were also less likely to work in dangerous jobs. It is still true today that life expectancy is generally longer in wealthier countries and for people with more money in those countries. Americans who live in poverty still, in the twenty-first century, have lower life expectancies.

In the United States, the life expectancies of African Americans and Native Americans have improved more slowly than those of white Americans. Until 1865, most African Americans were enslaved, forced to work and live in awful conditions, often subjected to unspeakable violence, and denied healthy food, well-ventilated homes and good medicine. After slavery ended, in many places, African Americans still confronted similar harsh realities of violence and were denied opportunities because of their skin color. This history matters, in part, because it continues to affect people alive today.

Doctors, clinics, clean water and medicine also came much more slowly to American Indian reservations, where Native Americans were forced, often violently, to move in the 1800s. Access to health care is still lower on some Native American reservations than in nearby areas. Being aware of these inequalities is the first step to changing them.

Our Genes

For certain diseases, if our parents or grandparents had them, we are more likely to get them; this is why doctors sometimes ask your parents about "family history" at check-ups. Many diseases, including cancers, if caught early, are treatable or even curable. That means that we may survive what took the lives of our grandparents—and live longer.

Our family history reveals some of what's in our genes. Our bodies are made up of trillions of tiny cells. Yes, trillions. That's more stars than there are in our whole galaxy! Each cell contains thousands of genes. Our genes determine whether we have curly hair or straight hair, whether we have brown eyes or green eyes, and our risk for certain diseases. Some illnesses are tied to specific genes (which is why it's good to know our family history). Other illnesses come from infections or are triggered by things in our environment (like pollution or secondhand cigarette smoke). We can't change our genes, but we can be aware of our family histories, go to our checkups, get our vaccines and make healthy choices every day, including eating a heart-healthy diet and exercising.

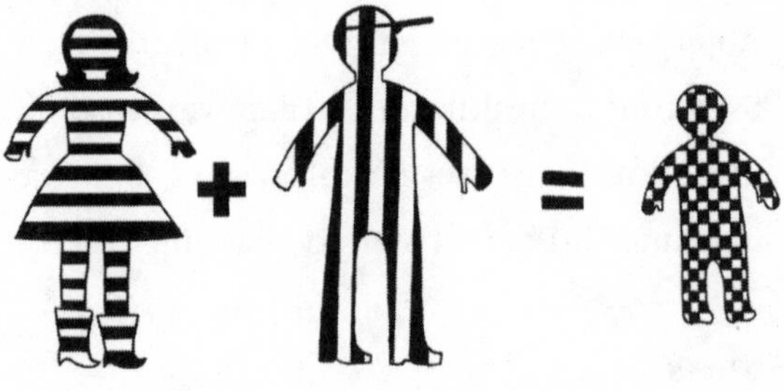

START NOW!

- Wash your hands (especially after you go to the bathroom, before you eat and if you're ever in a hospital)
- Make sure your vaccines are up-to-date (ask a parent, grandparent or your doctor)
- Learn to take your pulse
- Learn hands-only CPR through the American Heart Association—or ask your school to offer hands-only CPR classes
- Eat lots of veggies and fruits
- Don't eat lots of fried food, candy or sweets
- Drink water and avoid sugary soda
- Play actively one hour a day as often as you can
- Check out what's in your refrigerator/pantry/cabinet to see what's there and how healthy it is
- Count the ingredients on packaged food
- Encourage your family to buy healthy, nutritious food, including fresh and frozen fruits and vegetables
- Encourage friends and family to be more active
- Know your family's health history
- Write to your local elected officials to support access to healthy food and activities at your school and in your community

CHAPTER 4

FOOD, HUNGER AND WHY VITAMINS ARE AWESOME

Ever notice that your tears are salty? Same as the salt found in the oceans. Our bones and teeth are made of a mineral called calcium, same as what is found in seashells and chalk. We need iron to help our blood do its job of carrying oxygen from the tops of our heads to the tips of our toes. Same as the iron used to build buildings. But we don't snack on the shells we collect at the beach or chew on poles.

Salt, calcium and iron are only a few of the nutrients we need. What other nutrients are essential to keeping our vital organs healthy and our bodies strong? How do we get the nutrients we need? These are a couple of the questions we'll investigate in this chapter.

Macronutrients: The Fuel of Life

Carbohydrates, proteins and fats are called macronutrients. *Macro* means "large" and we need macronutrients in large amounts to be healthy. Carbohydrates give us energy. For most people around the world, carbohydrates, like those in vegetables, fruits, pasta, cereal and rice, are their main source of calories, or energy.

Proteins and fats are also important for fueling our bodies and helping our muscles grow. Muscles help us run and jump—they also help us sit and stand up straight, and even sleep! Our most important muscle is our heart and, like other muscles, it needs to be fed and exercised. Protein is important to our blood and to our immune system—it helps us fight off germs and get better if we get sick. Fat protects our vital organs.

Micronutrients: An Alphabet Soup

Ever wonder about the list on the side of a cereal box? While it may look like a mixed-up alphabet, it's made up mainly of micronutrients—vitamins and minerals that keep us healthy but that we don't need in as big amounts as we need macronutrients. *Micro* means "small"—the opposite of *macro*. Historically, we got vitamins mainly from fruits and vegetables. Now, we can also get vitamins from . . . vitamins!

Our bodies need lots of different vitamins to stay healthy. You may have heard of vitamin C. It's in oranges, lemons and other citrus fruits; it helps our immune system fight off infections and our bodies heal. Vitamin A is in orange foods like carrots and cantaloupe and in lots of green foods like spinach and kale. It's important for our vision. It helps us see at night and helps us see colors, particularly bright ones. There are lots of different B vitamins. Vitamin B_{12} keeps our red blood cells and nerves healthy—our nerves enable us to feel things, like if something is hot or cold or if it's soft or rough. It can be found in eggs, chicken, cheese, fish, milk and meat. Vitamin D helps our bones grow strong and can be found in many of the same foods that have vitamin B_{12}. These are only a few of what are called "essential vitamins and minerals."

Bad Nutrition

Bad nutrition is when we don't get enough nutrients. It's dangerous because if we don't get enough essential vitamins and minerals, we're likely to get sick. This can happen if we don't eat balanced meals—meals that include fruits and veggies and a good mix of carbohydrates and proteins and fats.

Think of your diet as a rainbow: The more colors we're eating from fruits and veggies, the healthier our diet is. Fries, candy (even if colorful!) and sugary sodas don't make a well-balanced meal—there aren't enough good nutrients in them, and they have too many calories for our bodies to use. Calories we don't use get turned into fat; too much fat isn't good for anyone.

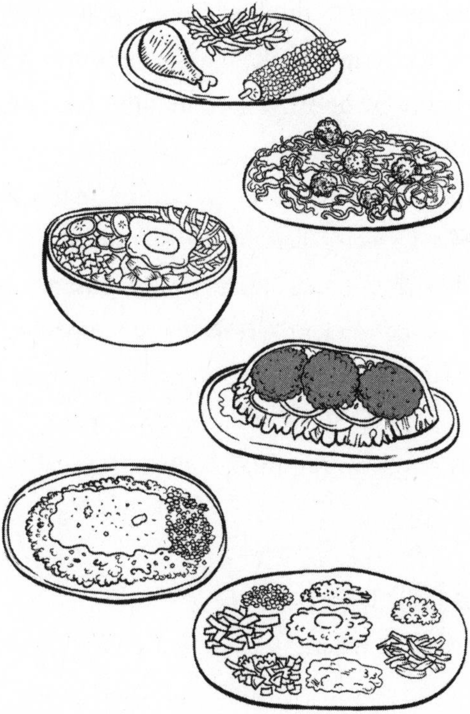

Hunger and Malnutrition

Hunger is different from bad nutrition. Hunger is our body's way of telling us we need to eat. If we go hungry over a long period of time, we become malnourished, and can starve. Malnutrition occurs when people do not eat enough food to give them the calories and nutrients they need to stay healthy. Even if they have enough of one type of food, if they're not getting enough of everything their bodies need, they could still be malnourished.

The opposite of malnutrition is called food security. It may sound strange to think of "food" and "security" in the same sentence, but it makes sense. If people have all the food needed to be healthy, they are more likely to be "safe" from illness or from hunger.

Starvation is extreme, even deadly, malnutrition. We really do need a well-balanced, healthy diet every day to live and be healthy. More than two thousand years ago, Hippocrates, an ancient Greek doctor, supposedly said to his students: "Let thy food be thy medicine and thy medicine be thy food." We now know that if we don't get the right nutrients from our food, we could actually *get* sick.

Vitamin C and Scurvy

In 1769, Dr. William Stark wanted to understand how the foods people ate related to their health. So, he experimented on himself to see what would happen if he only ate certain foods—it didn't turn out well. Dr. Stark first ate only bread and drank only water for thirty-one days. Then, he added foods back to his diet one at a time, including meat and milk. Two months after Dr. Stark began his experiment, he noticed his gums were red and swollen, signs of a disease called scurvy, which occurs when our bodies don't get enough vitamin C. A few months later, Dr. Stark died, likely of scurvy or malnutrition. Our bodies need vitamin C!

In Dr. Stark's time, scurvy was common among sailors because when ships were only powered by the wind (or people rowing), sea voyages often took many weeks or months. Sailors didn't get to eat fruits and vegetables between ports (because they would spoil—refrigerators hadn't been invented yet, or the electricity needed to power them!). Doctors who treated sailors and lived with them on board could observe what foods helped sailors stay healthier. One of those doctors, Dr. James Lind, found that oranges, lemons and limes seemed to treat and prevent scurvy. By the late 1700s, every ship in the British navy carried lime juice. Although no one knew yet what vitamin C was, Dr. Lind had figured out that whatever was in citrus fruits prevented the bleeding—and eventually death—caused by scurvy.

Vitamin A and Blindness

Thousands of years ago, ancient Egyptians found that kids who didn't eat a balanced diet might lose the ability to see clearly or even go blind. They treated night blindness (the inability to see at night) and other vision problems with liver—either by eating it or by squeezing liver "juices" directly into the eye (very glad we don't do that anymore!).

Many meats (including liver), eggs and green vegetables are rich in vitamin A. These are often the most expensive foods, which means they are hardest for people living in poverty around the world to buy. More than 250 million people suffer because they don't get enough vitamin A–rich food. It is the leading cause of blindness across the globe.

Vitamin K and Blood

If you get a scrape or small cut, you might notice that after a few minutes the bleeding stops, particularly if you press on the cut with a cotton ball or a Band-Aid. Bleeding stops because your blood clots—the blood actually gets thick and stops flowing. As it turns out, there's a vitamin that is important to clotting, and we can thank chickens for the discovery.

In 1929, Danish researcher Henrik Dam was studying chickens and what they ate. He discovered that chickens needed a special vitamin to help their blood clot. Without it, they would bleed to death from even a small wound. First named in a German scientific journal, the vitamin was called the "clotting vitamin," or *Koagulationsvitamin* in German. In English, it's shortened to vitamin K. For this discovery, Dr. Dam received a Nobel Prize in Medicine, one of the highest scientific honors.

We know now that vitamin K helps our blood to clot too. Whether we get a small paper cut or skin our knee, we need our blood to clot so the injury can heal. Green leafy vegetables like spinach, parsley and broccoli have lots of vitamin K.

Calcium and Bones

Minerals are solid substances that occur in nature; they're often found in rocks. For thousands of years, the mineral calcium was used in mortar, a type of glue used to stick bricks together. A mixture including calcium was used to build the Great Pyramid of Giza, in Egypt, and the Great Wall of China. It's the most common mineral in the human body, found in our teeth and bones. It also keeps our muscles, including the heart, working well.

Sometimes minerals and vitamins work together. Without vitamin D, our bodies can't use the calcium we eat or drink. That's why you may have noticed your milk is "fortified" with vitamin D, or has vitamin D added to it. Without enough calcium and vitamin D, we can develop rickets, which is a disease that softens bones. Rickets is very painful. It slows down bone and body growth and bends leg bones outward. More common in developing countries, rickets is very rare in the U.S. because most Americans get enough calcium from dairy products (milk, yogurt, cheese), green leafy vegetables, vitamin D–fortified foods and sunlight (yes, sunlight!).

Salt and Water

People have been eating salt forever. Thousands of years ago, in ancient Egypt, China and other places, salt was used in medicines, as a seasoning, and as a preservative. It kept food from spoiling (before refrigerators were invented). It is used in some religious ceremonies. Salt even appears in religious texts, including the Bible and the Quran.

Salt is so important that it has even been used as money! That's how we got the word *salary*, the payment people earn for doing a job. (Did you notice the first three letters in *salary* are the same as the first three letters in *salt*? Not an accident.) During the War of 1812, when the American government didn't have enough money to pay soldiers, it paid them in salt.

Salt has also been used as a weapon. Armies would "salt the earth," to prevent their enemy's crops from growing. This is because soil, like our bodies, needs a balance of minerals and water to be healthy—too much salt kills crops.

Salt is vital to our health. It helps our bodies digest other nutrients and supports our nervous system, which connects our brain to our body. In the right amount, it also helps our bodies maintain healthy blood pressure.

On a hot day or when we exercise, we sweat out water and salt. If we sweat too much without drinking enough water, we become dehydrated, and we need to replace both the water and salt our body lost. If you're thirsty, it could be because you're dehydrated or because you ate too much salt and you didn't drink enough water to balance it out.

Many Americans, including kids, eat more salt than we need, often by eating prepared foods high in "hidden" salt, like in breads, soups or sauces. We then need to drink more water to get back to a healthy balance of water and salt. It's good to try to eat less salt. We're less likely to get dehydrated at any point or have high blood pressure as we age.

Iron and Blood

Although the ancient Romans invented books (they were the first to stack pages and bind them together), concrete and advanced medicine, in many ways they were uncivilized and unjust. They enslaved people and had gladiators fight to the death for entertainment. They also had many unhygienic, or unsafe, practices, including drinking the blood of dead gladiators. Romans believed drinking blood from strong fighters (even if they'd lost the fight and their lives) would make their own blood strong and cure diseases. Some people who were ill even drank gladiators' blood straight from open scrapes or cuts. They were wrong about drinking blood, but right that they needed healthy blood in their bodies to survive.

Blood has long fascinated scientists. It was among the earliest things scientists studied under a microscope. One of the most important minerals for healthy blood is iron. The same iron used to make cars is key to building hemoglobin, the part of our blood that takes oxygen from our lungs and brings it to every part of our bodies.

If we don't get enough iron from meat, eggs, leafy green vegetables and other foods, we may develop anemia, which can make us weak and tired. Anemia gets its name from Greek and means "without blood." Too much iron is also dangerous and can make someone very sick. Making sure you have the right amount of iron is one of the reasons why many doctors have your blood tested during regular checkups.

Fat and Protein

When you hear "fat," what do you think? That it's bad? Or unhealthy? While too much fat is unhealthy, our bodies need fat. It protects our organs and nerves. Fat also helps our bodies absorb, or use, vitamins such as A, D and K. There are different types of fats. "Bad" fats, like those found in fatty meats or fried foods, increase cholesterol. "Good" fats don't, and they can be found in nuts, seeds, fish, avocado, coconut oil, olive oil, eggs and more.

Protein is sometimes called the building block of life. It's in every cell in our bodies. Protein helps us make new cells and heal damaged ones. It is particularly important in growing and repairing blood cells, muscles (including the heart) and tissue, which connects organs and other body parts together. (Note: This tissue is not like the tissue you use to blow your nose!) Protein also helps us fight off infection.

Red meat (like beef and goat meat), poultry (like chicken and turkey), seafood, beans, eggs and dairy products have the most protein. While we may not think of green vegetables as having protein, many do (like peas and broccoli). Eating "lean" protein means we'll get protein and "good" fat without too much "bad" fat.

We're lucky to live in a time when we know enough about the science of nutrition to know what to eat—and not eat—to be healthy. Thank you to Dr. Lind, Dr. Dam, Dr. Stark and countless others for discovering what essential nutrients are and where we can find them. As we think about how to fill our fridges and pantries with nutritious food, let's think about our neighborhoods, our towns, our country and our world. Do you think everyone has enough good, healthy food to eat?

Hunger

The sad answer to the last question is no. Everywhere in the world—including in the United States—people are hungry, even kids. In the U.S., one out of every six kids is hungry or worried about where their next meal will come from. Across the world, many millions more face hunger, and tragically, every year, children die because they don't get the nutrition they need to stay healthy, to thrive, to learn, to live.

In the United States, one out of every six kids is hungry. That means three out of every eighteen kids are hungry.

What Is Hunger?

Can you imagine being hungry all the time? Being painfully hungry? Every day? Maybe you don't have to imagine. Maybe you have been. I was very lucky as a kid to never have to worry about having enough nutritious food to eat.

We all know what hunger feels like if we skip breakfast or need to eat after soccer practice. Our stomachs may grumble or our heads may hurt, but those feelings will go away as soon as we eat. That's a different type of hunger than chronic malnutrition or chronic hunger, hunger that never goes away.

Chronic hunger is when someone doesn't have enough nutrients or calories over many days, even weeks, months or years. Around the world, some people are hungry because the crops they rely on for food got ruined because of a drought (not enough rain), a flood (too much water) or other natural disaster. Others go hungry every year between crop cycles, or the time when different crops are harvested. This is known as a "hunger season." Some people are hungry because wars in their country make it hard to grow or find enough food to eat. Some people are hungry because the food they eat may provide their bodies with enough calories but not with enough of the nutrients our bodies need, like calcium or iron.

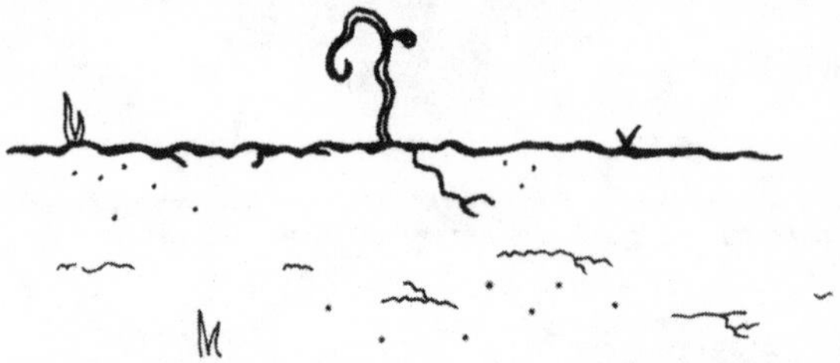

There is less hunger in the world today than there was even a few decades ago. The American scientist Dr. Norman Borlaug developed types of wheat that could grow in different places and survive nasty weather. People around the world use wheat to make different types of bread, cereal and pasta, so more wheat provides more food to more people. Some people believe Dr. Borlaug's work has saved hundreds of millions of lives. Yet there are close to 800 million people who are hungry around the world. Imagine if you lined up one hundred New York Citys next to one another. That's about 800 million people. Now imagine every single person who lives in all of them is hungry. It is a lot of people.

Most people are hungry because they don't have enough money to buy or grow the food they need. This is true even in places like the U.S. where food is not in short supply. The U.S. produces enough food to feed everyone, but not everyone gets the food they need and a lot of food goes to waste.

Who Is Hungry in the U.S.?

Men, women and children all over America are hungry. There are Americans who are hungry in cities and in the countryside, of every race and practicing any religion. Childhood hunger is very dangerous because it can hurt kids throughout their lives. You are growing right now, so now is the time when your body needs nutrients most. Kids who are hungry don't get enough nutrients for their brains to develop and it's harder for them to concentrate. Hunger also makes it harder to fight off infections, which means hungry kids are sick more often and for longer. All of that makes it tougher to go to school and to learn.

Many kids go to school hungry every day. For some, the school lunch may be their only daily meal. Many adults who are hungry work and work hard. Their jobs don't pay enough for them to buy enough healthy, nutritious food and for the other necessities in life (including a home). Some people who are hungry have disabilities that prevent them from working to earn money to buy food. No one should go hungry anywhere, particularly in the wealthiest country on Earth, the United States, but many, many do.

Tackling Hunger

Where do Americans who are hungry get food? Schools provide free or less-expensive lunches and breakfasts to kids from families who can't afford to pay the full price, or any price, for a meal. In many communities, food pantries, food banks or soup kitchens offer hungry people free meals. There are lots of ways to support food pantries, food banks and soup kitchens, including by donating money, food or time to volunteer (you may not be old enough to volunteer, but even if you can't go, you can encourage older family members to volunteer for you). Many Americans also rely on a government program which gives families living in poverty money to buy food. It's called SNAP (short for Supplemental Nutrition Assistance Program), though it is sometimes referred to as "food stamps."

In some communities, students are growing food to feed families. One day when she was in third grade, Katie brought home a cabbage seedling from a gardening program at her school in South Carolina. She planted it and watched it grow. The full-grown cabbage wasn't small—it was forty pounds, which is as heavy as some first graders! Katie knew that such a special cabbage needed a special home and so she donated it to a local soup kitchen, a place where people could go for a free cooked meal. That was just the first of many cabbages Katie donated. She persuaded her school to set aside land for a school garden. She then started an organization called Katie's Krops, which helps kids all over the country grow healthy food to donate to people in need. Today there are one hundred gardens run by kids in thirty-three states!

Photo courtesy of Katie's family

Katie with one of her giant cabbages

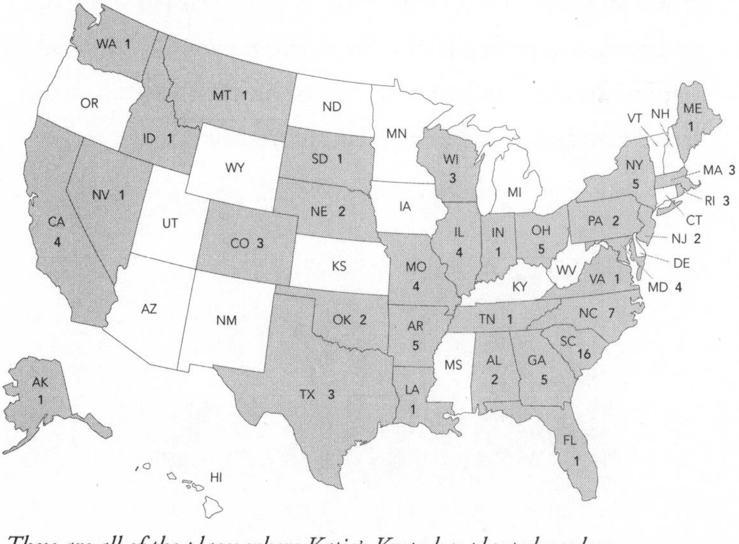

These are all of the places where Katie's Krops has planted gardens

Waste Not . . .

Restaurants and grocery stores also donate food to food pantries and other places hungry families may go, usually food that would go to waste. Close to half of all the food produced in the United States is thrown away, instead of eaten. You can help rescue some of it, anywhere you spend time where meals are served, including at school.

In Colorado at Douglass Elementary, a group of first through fifth graders called the Food Waste Club decided to teach their classmates how to cut down on food waste. The club led a "waste audit" to see what foods were and were not being eaten in the cafeteria. They found that many students threw away fruits and vegetables—without even trying them or touching them. So, in response, the club put out an "untouched food bin," where students can place uneaten fruits and vegetables. That food is later washed and then eaten by someone else. The Food Waste Club is now teaching students at neighboring schools what they can do to make sure good food gets eaten, not trashed.

Photo courtesy of Douglass Elementary

Students from the Food Waste Club

All of these programs are so important because nutrition is nutrition, no matter how you get it. There is no shame in buying food with SNAP or getting free lunch at school. Vitamin A, B, C, D or K doesn't know how it got into your body or how much the food it came in cost. The same is true with proteins or fats. If you're lucky enough to not worry about having enough food at home, encourage your family to send food or money to a food pantry, food bank or soup kitchen in your neighborhood. You can also start a food waste program or a school garden. Every bit of nutritious food, with all its vitamins and minerals, fats and proteins, matters.

START NOW!

- Know your nutrition and help educate your family about nutrition
- Start reading labels on food packages to see what exactly you're eating
- Identify what nutrients are in your favorite foods
- Create a rainbow of fruits and veggies on your plate during mealtimes
- Talk to your family about donating food you buy or grow to food banks
- Start a food drive at school—ask your classmates to bring in packages of food, like canned vegetables and bags of rice, that you can send to local food banks
- Fight food waste at school by starting a club like the Food Waste Club
- Start a school garden through Katie's Krops or another similar program
- Don't judge people for how they get their food
- Encourage older family members to volunteer at food banks, food pantries and soup kitchens

- Write to elected officials and ask what they are doing to help hungry people in your community, and share ideas of what more you think they should be doing so everyone can have enough healthy food to eat

CHAPTER 5

ALLIES, FRIENDS AND STANDING UP TO BULLIES

Have you ever been bullied? Chances are the answer may be yes. Every school year, one in five kids reports being bullied. That probably doesn't paint the full picture because many kids do not report bullying. They may feel ashamed, even though they shouldn't because being bullied is not their fault. Or maybe they are worried that bullies will be more vicious if the bullies know their bad behavior was reported.

Everywhere I go and meet with kids, they've talked to me about bullying. About how common bullying is at their school, about what they and their friends are doing to stand up to bullies and prevent bullying. About how scared they and their friends are that they might be bullied or bullied again. Often two kids would bravely stand up together to share their story and their anti-bullying efforts. They would talk about how one was bullied because he was gay, or because she was part of an immigrant family, or because they were both considered ugly. While their stories were painful, it was inspiring to see their demonstrations of being an ally, or actively supporting each other.

Why do bullies bully? How can we prevent and stop bullying? How can we support students who have been bullied and are standing up to bullies? Answering these questions is part of why I wrote this chapter. I also wanted to share stories of kids who are kind and brave in the face of bullying and who are working to create kinder and more respectful communities.

Types of Bullying

Bullying comes in many different forms. Verbal bullying is when a bully uses cruel words to harass or threaten someone. It can be mean teasing, name-calling and even threats of violence. Physical bullying is when a bully hurts someone by hitting, kicking, pinching, spitting, pushing, tripping, shoving or worse. Physical bullying also includes when someone's things are hurt—books torn or clothes ripped or a phone broken. Social bullying is when a bully spreads gossip or lies about someone. Embarrassing or threatening someone in front of other kids is also social bullying. So too is leaving someone out of plans or activities on purpose to be mean and hurt that person's feelings.

Physical, verbal and social bullying often happen in school, on the playground or on the bus to or from school. Verbal and social bullying also occur online, on social media, in group texts and chats and elsewhere. When bullying happens online, it's called cyberbullying. But bullying doesn't just happen around school or online. Bullying can, and does, happen anywhere kids are. That means bullying can happen at a church, synagogue or mosque, at a gym, playground or sports field, at a mall, a pool, a hockey rink or on a smartphone.

How Bullying Hurts

It's no fun being bullied—and it can be painful to our bodies, our hearts and our spirits. It can hurt how we feel about ourselves. Kids who are bullied over weeks, months or even years are more likely to be very sad and anxious, or very worried. Kids who are bullied can have horrible nightmares and lose sleep. This is true for kids who have been physically threatened or harmed—but it's also true for kids who have been verbally and socially bullied. Words can hurt—some kids who are verbally bullied say they feel sick to their stomachs a lot. Grades can drop because of how anxious kids who are bullied feel. Their anxiety makes it harder to study and pay attention in class. If what I've described feels like some things you've experienced, make sure you tell a parent, grandparent, teacher or other grown-up you trust and who can help.

Over time, kids who are bullied are likely to stop going to places where they're bullied. That's why kids who are bullied are more likely to drop out of school or quit sports teams. Kids who drop out of school are less likely to go back to school later and less likely to go to college. Adults who were bullied as kids are more likely to be unhappy and depressed—feeling very sad and hopeless—later in life. Being bullied in elementary school can affect someone's life forever. Being a bully can also be bad for someone's health. Bullies are more likely to be depressed and unhappy throughout their lives. Stopping bullying is good for the bullies' health too.

Why Do Bullies Bully?

Have you ever heard someone say bullying is a good way to act? I haven't. Not in school or out of school. I have heard people say "boys will be boys" or "don't take it so seriously" or "she was just teasing." But none of those excuse bullying or make it okay. So, why does someone bully? Some bullies may be scared, and being mean to someone else can help them feel, even for a moment, less scared and more powerful. Some bullies want attention—even negative attention. If kids are scared of them and teachers are punishing them, some bullies may think that's better than being ignored. Other bullies want to feel important by putting other kids down. For some bullies, all of those may be true. Bullying tells us something about the bully—meanness, cruelty, the fact that they don't feel good about themselves—not about the person being bullied. There are many explanations for why someone might bully.

Sadly, some kids grow up in homes where the adults often shout, are mean to each other and to kids, and may even be violent. Kids who grow up in homes where there's lots of mean language and violence may not understand how hurtful their insults or shoving or pushing around other kids can be—for them, it may be painfully normal.

Bullies are generally looking for a reaction—for someone

to get upset, to cry, to be in visible pain. It's hard not to be upset when a bully attacks. That old saying "Sticks and stones can break my bones but words will never hurt me" isn't always true.

Stand Up

It is important to stand up to bullies—though that's often easier said than done. Still, looking a bully directly in the eye and calmly saying, "I won't be bullied" doesn't give bullies the reaction they want. Not shouting, not backing away, not responding in anger all prove that bullies aren't going to get the power over you that they want. Experts say questioning what bullies are saying ("Why would you say that?") and using the bully's name while speaking firmly ("Stop it.") can help discourage bullies.

A bully tries to make victims seem not worthy as people—to make them feel like they are nothing more than a mean word about who they are or where they come from, their gender, their race, their religion, a disability, their family or their neighborhood. Don't let bullies do that.

If they don't get the reaction they want, they're more likely to move on to try to bully other victims. You can help your friends and classmates not be victims by practicing standing up to bullies. You can also stand up to bullies even if you're not the one being bullied. Part of a bully's plan is to shame the victim and make the victim feel alone and powerless. Being an ally, a friend, is a way to show bullies they won't succeed in isolating someone. More than half of bullying at schools stops when someone else—a friend or classmate—stands up to the bully.

After Bella was bullied in third grade, her parents encouraged her to stand up for herself. She did, and eventually the bullying stopped. When Bella was in fourth grade, she saw a boy with special needs being bullied. She knew she needed to do more than just stand up for herself. She needed to stand up for her classmates too. Bella realized most kids are bystanders, so she encouraged other kids to "stand-up and step-in" to end bullying. She came up with the "Three Cs" (Compassion, Confidence and twenty seconds of Courage) to help kids be allies to one another and stop bullying before it starts. Because of Bella's efforts, her school adopted a "Be A Buddy—Not A Bully" pledge. More important, Bella's school experienced less bullying and became a kinder community. Her efforts have inspired other kids and schools to adopt similar anti-bullying programs—and pledges.

When Bella or any kid stands up to a bully, that tells kids who have been bullied that they're not alone. Students who have been bullied say that their friends and classmates standing up for them made them feel better about themselves. Standing up to a bully also sends an important message to other kids nearby—it says, "This isn't okay. If we stand up to it, we have a chance to stop it." If no one stands up, kids who may not have made up their minds about the bullying or the bully may think it's okay. It takes a lot of courage and is very hard to do, but it helps to know you are not alone.

Tell a Trusted Adult

Standing up to bullies also means reporting them to teachers, principals, coaches, bus drivers and other adults in charge that you trust so they can help. Sometimes those same adults may not see what you see or hear what you hear. If you tell them what's happening, they can help stop the bullying and protect other kids from being bullied. If you see a bully physically threaten someone, ask a grown-up to help immediately. If you see a bully verbally abusing someone and you're not sure how to stand up, ask a trusted adult for advice. There is no shame in asking for help. Asking for help when you need it shows that you are strong and smart.

Bullies depend on kids not wanting to be "tattletales" or "snitches." It isn't snitching or telling tales to report something that has happened. It isn't gossiping to tell an adult that someone is bullying. Sometimes, it may take a while to explain social or cyberbullying to adults. The words you use in school today may not be the same words your parents used. The apps you may use in school or on a phone are probably not the apps your parents use. Not standing up to a bully or asking a trusted adult for help is making a choice to let the bullying continue.

Kindness

Bullying behavior can begin at any time—for some kids it's as early as preschool. How can we stop someone from becoming a bully? Or help a bully stop being a bully? One key is to show people kindness and respect.

Kindness creates more kindness. You can be kind by being considerate of what other people need and how they are feeling. That could mean smiling and asking how someone is doing, even if they're not nice to you. Or asking others to join in on the playground or at your study group at school. Being generous—sharing smiles, time, energy—is one of the ways we show kindness. Did you know that when students perform three acts of kindness a week, they're more likely to be accepting of others and less likely to bully? Recognizing and celebrating kindness is also important. We can do that by saying thank you when someone is kind to us or to someone else. Celebrating kindness spreads kindness—it encourages more people to be kind, and to be kind more often. That's true in school, at home, in clubs, on sports teams—pretty much everywhere.

Sometimes kindness starts with making sure no one is sitting alone. When seven-year-old Christian's family was planning a move to Germany for his dad's job, he was worried about being lonely. He had seen kids standing alone on the playground at his school in the U.S. and he worried that might be him in his new German school. One of the German schools his family considered had a program called the buddy bench. If a child was sitting alone on the bench, other kids would go and ask that kid to play. While Christian's family didn't end up moving to Germany, he brought the buddy bench idea to his American school, where his principal agreed to install one in the playground. Kids, including Christian, used it; it didn't sit empty, or with only one kid, for very long. Now there are buddy benches in all fifty states and in fourteen countries around the world! You can ask your teacher or principal about installing a buddy bench—it doesn't need to be a special kind of bench, just whatever works best for your school.

Photo courtesy of Christian's family

Christian sitting on a buddy bench

Being kind also means being kind to kids who have been bullies. It doesn't mean that their behavior is okay. It means understanding that a bully may not have experienced kindness or respect at home. You can show bullies something they may not have known before: a friendship based on kindness and shared positive experiences, in classrooms, cafeterias, on playgrounds and beyond school.

Respect

Like with kindness, respect creates more respect. Maybe you've heard the word *tolerance*. Tolerance is not the same as respect. If we get a cold, we tolerate our runny noses and itchy eyes—we deal with it, even if we don't like it. If we respect one another, that means we recognize that another person is valuable for who they are. That they, like us, have equal dignity and equal rights—to be in school, on the playground, on the sports field, everywhere. We respect one another—we don't just tolerate one another.

We can show respect for our friends and neighbors by

creating ways for everyone to participate. When she was in third grade, Rachel realized that some children with special needs couldn't play on the playground. She thought everyone deserved a chance to play together. Rachel also worried that kids with special needs were more likely to get made fun of, or be bullied. Rachel decided her Kentucky town needed a new playground that all kids could use, which would also prevent bullying (because the kids would be playing together and supporting one another). She started raising money for it, in part by designing and selling T-shirts. Four years later, the Fun for Everyone playground is finally open! There are playgrounds that all kids can use across the country—but not everywhere. Maybe you can help start one, if there isn't one near you!

Photo courtesy of Rachel's family

Rachel at the site of her Fun for Everyone playground

Playing together helps us get to know one another. Talking to each other helps too. Bullies are less likely to bully people they know and are less likely to bully kids who are their friends. They're also less likely to bully other kids who have lots of friends. Also, kids with good friends are less likely to bully others.

Some Kids Might Get Bullied More

Bullies can be girls, boys, of any religion or any race, from any school, anywhere. Kids who are bullied are equally diverse. Still, some kids are more likely to be bullied than others. Most kids who have been bullied report that the bullies used their looks as an excuse to be mean. Children of color, children from immigrant families that came to America from other countries, children with special needs, Muslim children, children whose families live in poverty, children who are girls, overweight children and LGBTQ children are all more likely to be teased and threatened—to be bullied. (*LGBTQ* stands for lesbian, gay, bisexual, transgender and queer or questioning.)

More than half the kids who reported being bullied in a year said the bullies used their weight as an excuse to be mean and cruel. Bullying someone for their weight is called "fat shaming." Unfortunately, it is still legal in the United States to discriminate against—or treat someone differently—because of their weight. That doesn't make it right—and it shouldn't happen in school or anywhere. *Fat* is not a bad word. Standing up to bullying means standing up to fat shaming.

African American kids are more likely to be bullied than white kids in schools. One in four African American children reports being verbally, physically or socially bullied in a school year because of the color of their skin. Treating people cruelly because of the color of their skin is a clear form of racism. Racism, like any form of prejudice, is not an opinion. An opinion is if you like blue and your friend likes green. Or you like one sports team and your friend likes another. People may have opinions about all sorts of things, but thinking that one person is better than another because of their race is not the same as liking one sport more than another or liking plain peanut butter sandwiches more than peanut butter and jelly sandwiches.

After a bully harassed ten-year-old Kheris because of her dark skin, her sister, Taylor, shared a photo of her on social media that went viral—tens of thousands of people saw it and liked it. They shared their support for Kheris by liking the post and sending supportive comments. The sisters thought no one should be bullied for their skin color. They started a T-shirt company with the slogan "Flexin' In My Complexion" to show their pride in their skin color and to encourage

Photo courtesy of Kheris's family

Kheris in her T-shirt

other kids to feel proud too. Their T-shirts also offered a way for other students to be supportive and prove that Kheris wasn't alone and that the bully was outnumbered.

In America, there is freedom of religion, which means anyone can practice any religion they want—or practice no religion at all. Sadly, that freedom doesn't protect kids from being bullied because of what other kids think about their faiths.

Muslims practice a religion called Islam, and Muslim children are more likely to be bullied than students of other religions. Treating Muslims worse or talking about Muslims or Islam in a negative way is called Islamophobia (iz-LAHM-uh-FO-bee-uh). Muslim girls who wear headscarves to school report their headscarves have been pulled, yanked, even taken off. Muslim elementary school students report being called awful, hateful names much more than students of other religions.

Jewish students also report being bullied more than Christian students do. Treating Jewish kids worse or talking about Jewish kids or Judaism in a mean, hateful way is called anti-Semitism (AN-tie-SEM-ih-tiz-im). Reaching out to Muslim and Jewish friends and classmates so they know they're not alone is something we can all do to prevent bullying. It shows our friends and classmates we stand with them if they are bullied.

We can do the same for our LGBTQ friends and classmates. No kid should be bullied because of who they are or who they love. People love in different ways. Words like *gay* and *lesbian* are not insults. It's not okay to use them to imply, or suggest, something bad. Similarly, someone's gender shouldn't be an insult. "You throw like a girl" shouldn't be a put-down for boys (or girls). "That's not what real boys wear" shouldn't be a put-down either. We should all wear what makes us feel good.

No kid should be bullied because of who loves them. Sometimes people have two moms, sometimes people have two dads, sometimes people have a mom and a dad, and sometimes people have one parent or aren't raised by their parents at all. Someone's family isn't a reason to bully or tease them. There are all kinds of people in this world, and all kinds of families, and no type of loving family is better than any other.

Cyberbullying

Adults sometimes think cyberbullying—whether on a phone or on a computer—isn't as serious as verbal bullying at school. It absolutely is. Meanness and cruelty are mean

and cruel wherever they happen. You may not be spending that much time online yet, but as you get older you will, and it's important to know about cyberbullying and how to stand up to cyberbullies.

Online, girls are more likely to be bullied than boys. Kids who are bullied online can be as hurt and frightened as those bullied in school. It's both easier and harder to stand up to bullies online. It's easier because you can erase mean messages and dismiss the bullying as not worth your time. If the online bully bullies more, you can keep erasing it.

It may also be harder to stand up to bullies online because it's not always clear who is sending hateful notes—bullies may use fake names. It's important to tell an adult you trust as soon as you experience or see cyberbullying so that they can help figure out who is doing the bullying. Cyberbullying is often done by groups of kids rather than one single kid. Once the bully or bullies have been identified, the adult, or you and the adult, can stand up to the bully, saying it's not okay to treat someone disrespectfully, online or off.

At times, verbal or cyberbullying is originally more subtle, or harder to detect. Some examples of this are when a bully might say "You're pretty for a Latina" or "You're a good baseball player for a gay guy" or "You're good at math for a girl" or "You're nice for an immigrant." None of those statements need anything after the *for*. If you think someone is pretty or a good athlete, smart or nice—pay them the compliment and give them the respect of making it about them, not about their race, their gender, their religion, who they love or where they were born.

Studies say that bullying is decreasing—but one in five kids bullied every year is still far too high. Even one kid bullied is too many. No one wants to be that kid.

Bullying thrives in shadows. We can deny bullies those shadows by bringing their actions to light. We can make it clear that respect is not reserved for people of one race or gender, or people from only one country or religion, or people who love in only one way. We can stop bullying by standing up to bullies and making clear there is no place for meanness and cruelty in our schools or anywhere. We can prevent bullying by being kind and respectful to one another and expecting kindness and respect in response. We can end bullying.

Our Shared Future

Standing up to bullying helps stop something bad from happening and it helps protect the health of our friends, our school and our community. By taking care of one another, we also take care of ourselves. Taking care of our Earth is part of caring for ourselves and one another too. We can start anytime we want—we can start now to make a positive difference in our own lives, for our friends, for our planet and for our shared future.

START NOW!

- Be kind
- Be respectful
- Practice standing up to bullies with your friends and trusted adults
- Stand up to bullies and ask for help when you need it
- Tell a trusted adult if bullying is happening at your school
- Reach out to people who may be at risk of being bullied so they know they're not alone
- Support friends and classmates who have been bullied
- Support accessible, inclusive playgrounds for all kids
- Read and share books and watch movies, television shows and videos with kind heroes
- If you think your school could use a buddy bench, ask your teacher or principal to install one
- Expect everyone in your life to treat others with kindness and respect and tell them when you think they could be more kind and more respectful

Acknowledgments

Thank you to all the people who helped bring this book to life, including Jill Santopolo, my extraordinary editor; Siobhán Gallagher, whose wonderful illustrations are throughout *Start Now!*; and the whole team at Penguin Young Readers and Philomel. Specifically, Jen Loja, Jocelyn Schmidt, Talia Benamy, Ellice Lee, Jennifer Chung, Theresa Evangelista, Kristie Radwilowicz, Sam Falconer, Cindy Howle, Rob Farren, Anne Heausler, Chandra Wohleber, Amy Hall, David Briggs, Wendy Pitts, Shanta Newlin, Lizzie Goodell, Emily Romero, Erin Berger, Rachel Cone-Gorham, Felicity Vallence, Christina Colangelo, Carmela Iaria, Venessa Carson, Felicia Frazier, Debra Polansky, the entire Penguin Young Readers sales team, Helen Boomer, Amanda D'Acierno and Dan Zitt. Thank you all.

Ruby Shamir provided invaluable research support, particularly in helping highlight remarkable young people doing remarkable work to help their families be healthier, our communities be stronger and our world be more sustainable; thank you, Ruby. To Haile, Joshua-Jadin, Keymar, Caleb, Katie, the Food Waste Club, Action4Air, Felix, Matti, Isiah, Devin, Roldan, Rhiannon, Madison, Bella, Kheris, Christian, Rachel and all your parents, thank you for allowing me to highlight your work and, even more, thank you for all you have done and are doing to help our world be healthier, more sustainable, more respectful and kinder.

I am particularly grateful to all the kid readers who read earlier drafts and provided terrific feedback. *Start Now!* is a better book because of Henry Karre, Amelia Horan, Ariel Feldman, Stella Luna, Jordan Bender, Nina Tavani, William Held, Olive Yoo and Wren Salane.

My wonderful team—Bari Lurie, Joy Secuban and Emily Young—makes all I do possible and I am grateful every day to work alongside each of them. My husband supports me in all I do and I am so thankful Marc is my partner in life, love and parenting. Most of all, thank you, Charlotte and Aidan, for inspiring me every day.

Index

D

E

O

P

R

S

T

V

W

Photo courtesy of the author

Chelsea Clinton is the author of #1 *New York Times* bestselling *She Persisted: 13 American Women Who Changed the World*; *She Persisted Around the World: 13 Women Who Changed History*; *It's Your World: Get Informed, Get Inspired & Get Going!* and, with Devi Sridhar, *Governing Global Health: Who Runs the World and Why?* She is also the Vice Chair of the Clinton Foundation, where she works on many initiatives, including those that help to empower the next generation of leaders. She lives in New York City with her husband, Marc, their daughter, Charlotte, their son, Aidan, and their dog, Soren.

You can follow Chelsea Clinton
on Twitter @ChelseaClinton
or on Facebook at www.facebook.com/chelsea clinton